SUMO Your Relationships

SUMO Your Relationships

How to handle not strangle the people you live and work with

by Paul McGee

Illustrations by Fiona Griffiths

CAPSTONE

BICENTENNIAL
1807
WILEY
2007
BICENTENNIAL

First published 2007 by:
Capstone Publishing Ltd. (a Wiley Company)
The Atrium, Southern Gate, Chichester, PO19 8SQ, UK.
www.wileyeurope.com
Email (for orders and customer service enquires): cs-books@wiley.co.uk

Reprinted July 2007

Other Wiley Editorial Offices
John Wiley & Sons Inc., 111 River Street, Hoboken, NJ 07030, USA
Jossey-Bass, 989 Market Street, San Francisco, CA 94103–1741, USA
Wiley-VCH Verlag GmbH, Boschstr. 12, D-69469 Weinheim, Germany
John Wiley & Sons Australia Ltd, 42 McDougall Street, Milton, Queensland 4064, Australia
John Wiley & Sons (Asia) Pte Ltd, 2 Clementi Loop #02–01, Jin Xing Distripark, Singapore 129809
John Wiley & Sons Canada Ltd, 22 Worcester Road, Etobicoke, Ontario, Canada M9W 1L1
Wiley also publishes its books in a variety of electronic formats. Some content that appears in print may not be available in electronic books.

Library of Congress Cataloging-in-Publication Data

McGee, Paul, 1964-
 SUMO your relationships : how to handle, not strangle, the people you live and work with / Paul McGee.

    p. cm.
Includes index.
ISBN 978-1-84112-743-9 (pbk. : alk. paper)
1. Interpersonal relations. 2. Social interaction. I. Title.
HM1106.M42 2007
158.2--dc22

                                                                    2007012097

Anniversary Logo Design: Richard J. Pacifico

Set in Meridien by Sparks (www.sparks.co.uk)
Printed and bound in Great Britain by TJ International Ltd, Padstow, Cornwall

This book is printed on acid-free paper responsibly manufactured from sustainable forestry in which at least two trees are planted for each one used for paper production. Substantial discounts on bulk quantities of Capstone Books are available to corporations, professional associations and other organizations. For details telephone John Wiley & Sons on (+44) 1243–770441, fax (+44) 1243 770571 or email corporatedevelopment@wiley.co.uk

'He who gets wisdom loves his own soul;
he who cherishes understanding prospers'

The Book of Proverbs:
Chapter 19 verse 8

Contents

SUMO Appreciation

The great thing about writing a book is the opportunity it provides to put into print your appreciation for countless people – so here goes.

Firstly, to my wise friend and mentor, Mr Sandham. Your humour, insight and honesty have been my bedrock for so many years – cheers bud – where would I be without you?

Secondly, I'd like to thank my family. Mum, you're an inspiration and you've taught me so much about the art of dealing with people. Dad, I guess my desire to tell stories and make people laugh is down to you – I just hope I've got better hearing than you when I'm older! Andy, my brother – we've shared a lot together – thanks for showing me above all the power and importance of listening. Thankfully though, I learnt my time management and organisational skills elsewhere.

Matt and Ruth – you make me immensely proud. Hopefully with the education and insights I've given you both, you'll also make me immensely rich one day. Seriously though – thanks for coping with my imperfections and complete lack of technical ability or sense of direction – you've got a lot to thank your Mum for.

As for Helen, my wife of nearly twenty years – what can I say? Quite a lot actually, as you well know. But I'll be brief for once. I'm not sure if I agree with Forrest Gump or not – life to me seems more like a roller coaster than a box of chocolates – I'm just so glad that my best mate has been with me for the ride. Thanks Babes.

Thirdly, I'd like to thank the people who took time to read through this book in its draft stage. Paul Sandham, Tom Palmer, Jeanie Donnell-Jones and Gail Bohin, your insights were invaluable – you challenged and stretched me and this book is richer because of your support. You're all stars.

Fiona Griffiths, you're a brilliant illustrator and an absolute joy to work with. I admire both your creativity and persistence in developing the SUMO characters – you always deliver. Thank you.

And finally thanks to the team at Capstone – John, Iain, Kate, Scott, Grace and Felicity – just make sure this book becomes a bestseller – and I guarantee you VIP tickets at Bradford City.

With appreciation,

Paul – The SUMO Guy

Introduction

It's said that money makes the world go round. That might be the case, but so do relationships.

Those of us living in the 21st century are likely to meet more people in one day than most people living in medieval times met in a lifetime. Admittedly, some of those encounters may be quite brief and superficial and probably don't deserve to be referred to as a relationship. For instance, I'm on nodding terms with a couple of people who serve me at the Post Office, but I would hesitate to use the term 'relationship' as a way of describing what goes on between us (even though Deirdre does give me my book of first class stamps with a certain twinkle in her eye). However, what begins as a brief encounter with someone may lead to something long term. (Not with you though, Deirdre.)

It's these longer term encounters that I want to focus on in this book. And I want to attempt what few books on this subject normally do – focus on relationships both in and outside the workplace. In my experience, both are crucial and our sense of fulfilment and happiness are inextricably linked to the quality of these relationships. Performance at work can be hindered or enhanced by how well we relate to a boss, colleague or customer. And in your personal life, the source of great joy or sorrow usually stems from your relationships with those closest to you.

What if you're feeling fairly satisfied with the quality of your relationships at the moment? Great. Congratulations. But join me anyway. Personally when it comes to dealing with people, I'm up for any help I can get, even if the journey so far has been going relatively well. In my experience, the ride isn't always smooth and sometimes we're not aware of what's around the corner.

But maybe you have been drawn to this book because you want to learn how to avoid strangling the people in your life. Okay, the word 'strangle' is perhaps a little extreme, but you get my point. Let me manage your expectations. I'm not promising you quick, superficial answers. And please be clear on this – your relationships won't improve because you've read this book. That will only happen when you start to apply and engage with the insights that are relevant to you. I'm talking about a partnership here, not a passive experience of reading some words on a page and then forgetting all about it.

This is serious stuff. Purely on a commercial level, this book could be worth thousands to you. Clients, customers and staff are all won and lost based around how good or bad we are at relating to each other. If that's what you gain from this book, then I'm happy for you. But I believe you could gain some insights that you'll struggle to put a monetary value on – but which will be priceless. Perhaps a marriage that seemed dead will be resurrected or a wounded relationship with a loved one may see the healing process begin. Maybe rather than saying 'I don't know what's got into him or her recently', you'll begin to find new ways of understanding others.

And at this point, let me clarify something regarding the title of this book – *SUMO Your Relationships*. The phrase SUMO – Shut Up, Move On – is sometimes misunderstood as it can sound rather aggressive to some people. Well, if you've read my previous book, *SUMO – Shut Up, Move On*, you'll understand what is at the very heart of the SUMO message. If not:

The phrase SUMO is split into two parts. 'Shut Up' means to take time out, to be quiet, to do some reflecting. We do so many things on auto pilot, i.e. without consciously thinking about what we're doing. Life is busy. People are in a hurry. We want everything now. The only thing is, we don't always take time to decide what we *really* want. This book gives you the chance to do so in terms of the relationships in your life. Appendix A gives a brief overview of the 'Six SUMO Principles' covered in my previous book and how they relate to this whole subject of relationships.

Unlike many books that explore how to deal with other people, I'll also be challenging you to examine yourself and reflect on your own behaviour and attitudes. Hard as it might be to imagine, it's just possible that someone bought this book with you in mind.

To help this process and to encourage you to stop and think, I include sections called 'SUMO pit stop's. Just like in a Formula One motor race, I'm encouraging you to leave the circuit temporarily in order that you're in a better position to complete it. It's an opportunity to refuel and perhaps, just as race conditions change and necessary adjustments need to be made, the SUMO pit stops provide you with an opportunity to consider what adjustments you need to make in order to improve your relationships.

However, I don't want to take the analogy too far. Life is not a race. It's not about winners or losers. I'm not encouraging you to view life as some competition where you're trying to get ahead of others. My approach is that we all learn or perhaps re-learn some ideas that enhance our relationships and ultimately make winners of us all.

And in case you're wondering – the 'Move On' part of SUMO is **not** another way of saying 'move out' or 'move away'. It's not a call to give up on people, or move on to a different relationship – that's not the essence of the 'move on' message. But although it's not the essence, it can sometimes be the reality. There may be occasions when it seems our only option is to literally let go and 'move on' – but I'm encouraging you to see this as your final option, not your first. Too often I feel I look for the quick way out. It's the easy option – but 'easy' doesn't always mean 'best'. As we'll see, improving relationships takes time, but – as I've seen from my own experience – it's time worth taking.

The 'Move On' message of SUMO is above all about hope. You can move on and things can change. You don't have to accept the current state of your relationships. The future can be different – if you want it to be.

Am I an eternal optimist? No. I'm realistic enough to recognise that things don't always move on in the way we would want. As I write, a close friend of mine has started divorce proceedings. Her marriage is now over, almost before it had begun. Her pain is tangible. The ending of her relationship is not by 'mutual agreement'. It's a story that will be echoed by many.

Equally, the workplace contains people so disaffected by their work that there seems little hope of change. But I remain an optimistic realist. I don't accept that such scenarios – although common – are always inevitable. Change can happen, but we may need a few more tools to help turn hopes into realities.

In writing this book and reflecting on my own character, I asked myself the question, 'Flawed, Fraud or Faithful?' My answer? All three.

To be honest, I do believe I'm flawed – in fact, I believe we all are to some extent. And yes I do sometimes feel a fraud as I fail to always practice what I preach. But when I'm being kinder to myself I also know that there are times when I'm being faithful to the values and principles I hold dear.

I guess this view of myself is a struggle many of us battle with – particularly in the context of our relationships. But I'm comforted by the words of the author and journalist Philip Yancey who wrote, 'We are all in peril if the flawed messenger invalidates the message.' I sincerely hope my own personal failings don't undermine the power of the message.

And as for my message, my close friend and mentor Paul Sandham said to me recently, 'If you haven't lived it or breathed it, don't write it.' I can assure you, I've taken on board his advice – you'll be reading plenty about my own personal encounters with people.

I think we all experience highs and lows in our relationships – I certainly have. But here's my perspective on what has made my own personal journey a little less bumpy than it might have been. It's based upon over twenty years of research, but perhaps more importantly, over forty years of life experience.

So determine, as you read this book, to learn from my mistakes as well as from my successes and work at making your journey and that of others, a little more comfortable as a result.

Enjoy the ride

Paul McGee – The SUMO Guy

P.S. If this book belongs to you (as opposed to being borrowed), you'll find the following helpful. To get the most from your read, have a pen, pencil or highlighter to hand. You'll be asked to reflect on a number of questions throughout the book, and I think on occasions you'll find it invaluable to write down your thoughts. There will also be certain stories or phrases that you come across and won't want to forget. I suggest you highlight them. Reading this book is about making a difference to your relationships, not about seeing how pristine you can keep the pages. But if you really can't bring yourself to do this, then please at least have a note book to hand whilst you're reading.

Welcome to Part One

In the first part of the book, we'll be focusing on Seven SUMO Realities. As the title suggests, there are some realities and basic assumptions about life and relationships that we need to be aware of. We're not dealing with people in isolation or in a vacuum – there's a variety of factors that interplay and connect with each other which we need to explore. Once we've done that, we can go on to learn more about relating more effectively to people.

If you're going to get the most out of this book, I urge you not to race through this section – it's packed with valuable insights that will help inform and illuminate the later material. When you're building a house, you've got to make sure you build solid foundations and that they go deep enough – the same is true with relationships. The Seven SUMO Realities are the foundations for the rest of the book.

Right, well, if you're sitting comfortably, let's begin with the first SUMO Reality.

Reality Rules

The reality of dealing with people

When it comes to operating machinery I'm no expert. If there's something wrong with my car, I'll open the bonnet with some vague misplaced notion that by doing so, the problem will in some magical way resolve itself. It never does. But if I had the time and inclination I guess I could read a manual and perhaps with a little help be able to fix the odd minor problem. (Indeed, after years of coaching and support I have learnt how to refill my windscreen washer bottle.) As for the more major tasks, a visit to the garage will normally suffice. The garage has both the equipment and expertise to carry out the work. And if the car is beyond repair? Simple – write it off and sell it for scrap.

This is all well and good when dealing with cars, but it's not quite that simple when it comes to dealing with people problems.

People are different. Relationships are complex. Although there are hundreds of books on the subject of relationships, there is no definitive guide on how best to manage them. Follow three simple steps on changing your spark plugs and, *hey presto*, it's sorted out. Follow three simple steps on how to deal with people and the outcome is less certain. There are dozens of different makes of car on the planet – but there are over six billion people. And despite our many similarities, each person is a unique individual. An effective approach on how to deal with a colleague at work or your partner at home may bring about positive results on Tuesday, but try the same approach on Thursday and stand back and watch the sparks fly. Enthusiasm and receptiveness one day: resentment and resistance the next.

Why?

Well, we're about to explore some of the multitude of reasons why people respond the way they do to situations. The key is to remember that although there will be lots of ideas and insights to help you build better relationships with others, this is not a quick fix manual. Reality rules. Events will happen that you hadn't expected. You'll respond to a person in a way you hadn't planned. Minor problems will escalate into major ones and you'll be left wondering, 'Where did it all go wrong?'

Welcome to life – a mixture of joy, excitement, the ordinary, the unusual, sadness, happiness, dreams, despair, success, setbacks – and all these experiences involve people. You see, there is no simple three step formula guaranteed to succeed every time. No magic cure. The perfect relationship doesn't exist. Reality rules.

> **SUMO wisdom**
>
> How many people do you know who have successfully completed the course 'How to lose friends and alienate people'?

Hope does exist

However, in the midst of the reality of our circumstances, new possibilities also exist. Things can change. Tomorrow can be different from today. Yes things can get worse, but they can also improve. Some 'realities' are not, in fact, permanent. They exist due to poor choices, a lack of awareness, a breakdown in communication – and the good news is all these can change.

> **SUMO wisdom**
>
> I may not be able to change the past, but I can influence the present and in doing so, create a more positive future.

So before we delve into some of the insights and strategies that can help us, let's remind ourselves of some of the realities we need to be aware of when dealing with relationships.

Here are some realities to be aware of

- Things in people's past (that neither they or you may be aware of) will influence their current behaviour.

  Which means that ... you may never discover the root cause of the behaviour, but you will be aware of its current impact.

- People's emotions fluctuate – sometimes for reasons that are not obvious.

  Which means that ... people do not respond consistently to situations.

- Not everyone is blessed with 'emotional intelligence' (see the work of Daniel Goleman).

  Which means that ... whereas some people seem naturally gifted in developing interpersonal relationships with others, some find this a huge challenge. What is common sense to one person could feel very unnatural to someone else.

- Some people lack self awareness. They don't reflect on their own behaviour or understand the impact their emotions have upon them. They fail to recognise their strengths and weaknesses or the impact their behaviour has on others.

  Which means that ... some of the most challenging people you live or work with are blissfully unaware of the impact they're having on you.

- We see in others the faults most prevalent in ourselves.

  Which means that ... we need to resolve issues with ourselves before we can resolve them with others.

- Titles don't equate to talent. Just because your job title is 'Manager' doesn't mean you can manage people.

Which means that ... it's what happens in practice rather than what's stated on paper that gives a true reflection of your ability to deal with people.

The most important reality of all — it takes two to tango

When it comes to dealing with what we may perceive as difficult people, the temptation can often be to focus on how we can fix the other person. Perhaps in our eyes they are solely responsible for the challenges we're facing – change them and you fix the problem. Wrong. The reality is usually very different. As they say, 'It takes two to tango.' If you're experiencing difficulties in any kind of relationship, the blame or problem is not solely with one party. I'm not suggesting there is equal responsibility, but we delude ourselves if we believe we are the completely innocent party. That's what we'll be focusing on throughout this book – the problems are not with 'them' – they're with 'us'. Recognise this reality and you're more likely to improve your relationships.

The personal stuff

I can relate to the reality 'we see in others the faults most prevalent in ourselves'. Ouch. Untidiness and collecting clutter seem to be talents I was born with. The phrase 'a place for everything and everything in its place' is a total anathema to me. And yet I detest with a passion clutter and untidiness. I work hard at overcoming my own weakness in this area, and over the years have achieved some minor victories – but it remains an ongoing battle. It's a trait within my personality that I struggle with. Interestingly, the 'untidiness and collecting clutter gene' is also prevalent in my wife, Helen, and daughter, Ruth. But unlike me they seem reasonably comfortable living life with it. Their tolerance to domestic chaos (as I perceive it) is far higher than my own. What I dislike within myself I also see so clearly within Helen and Ruth. It's been a source of stress to me which has lead to some fall-outs – I've not always responded appropriately. I guess the frustrations I have with myself in this area are then projected onto two people who are very close and very special to me. Bizarre, isn't it? But can you identify with my behaviour?

The work stuff

I was asked recently to spend some time coaching a newly promoted manager who was struggling to interact constructively with her team. Susan's emails were abrupt and considered aggressive by those receiving them. She struggled to maintain eye contact when talking to you. It never occurred to Susan to engage with people at a social level. She even felt that asking someone 'How was your weekend?' was intrusive. If a member of staff was performing poorly, her approach was either to ignore the problem or to confront the person publicly in the full view of other colleagues.

She confessed, 'I don't really like people much', and yet her knowledge of the job (which involved analysing and interpreting data) was exceptional.

Although I was happy to provide some ideas and strategies to help Susan, I felt this was a clear example of 'Reality Rules'. Susan was simply not 'wired' to engage with people at a level that others would consider normal. Could she improve? Yes. Would it be worth all the time and effort to do so? Probably not. Susan was brilliant with figures, but awful with people.

I advised her manager to create a new role for Susan that didn't involve her having to manage people. She flourished in her new role as Technical Consultant and her team responded brilliantly to her replacement – a manager with less technical expertise, but with high levels of emotional intelligence.

Some people have the social skills of Genghis Khan.

SUMO
wisdom

Experience counts

Even though I believe I have some natural skills when dealing with people, a lack of experience and the innocence of youth brings with it its own realities, as the following illustrates:

The work stuff

It was my big day. Finally I got to manage a team – thirty women who were working on the beefburger line in a frozen food factory. I'd spent four years at university. My degree involved studying psychology. I'd trained to be a probation officer and dealt with a number of young offenders – I was qualified and I was prepared. Managing thirty women would, I thought, be quite straightforward. I was 24 years old, had just completed my two-week induction programme and I was ready. This would be easy.

I was wrong. Very wrong. During my first week, they convinced me that. in order to leave work on time. they'd have to finish five minutes early in order to collect their coats from the cloakroom – which was a five minute walk from the production line.

My first experience managing a team was not a stunning success. The reality was, my academic background had not prepared me in the way I had hoped – qualifications were not the same as wisdom, commonsense and experience. After a week, I felt ready to quit. I was in at the deep end and I was struggling to stay afloat. I needed help. I learnt you cannot cram twenty years of experience into a two-week training programme. Reality rules.

SUMO pit stop

- Think about two key people in your work life and two in your personal life with whom you'd like to improve your relationship. Review the list 'Realities to be aware of'. Which of these is most helpful in understanding some of the key people in your life? Are your expectations of these people realistic?

- Reflect on the reality of 'It takes two to tango.' In what ways may your behaviour be contributing to some of your relationship challenges? Which realities about yourself do you need to be aware of?

Your SUMO takeaway

The context of our relationship challenges is that reality rules – people are the most complex creatures on the planet. Emotions will at times overrule logic, our past does influence our present and conflict is, at times, inevitable.

Further realities we have to accept if we're to avoid strangling people are:

- Some people lack common sense regarding relationships.

- People can be blissfully unaware of their impact on others.

- We see faults in others that we dislike within ourselves.

- It takes two to tango – relationship challenges are not down to one single person, we need to honestly examine our own contribution to the situation.

- Managing thirty women on the economy beefburger line is not easy.

Shut Up searching for superficial solutions to complex problems.
Move On to recognising Reality Rules.

SUMO
wisdom

My SUMO takeaway from 'Reality Rules' is ...

S.U.M.O. TAKEAWAY

$$E + R = O$$

Several years ago, Steve, a friend of mine lent me a set of tapes called *Self Esteem and Peak Performance* by Jack Canfield (now known by many for being the co-author of the *Chicken Soup for the Soul* series). Listening to the tapes in the car, I was half-way through my journey when Canfield began to elaborate on the principle 'E + R = O'. I admit that what he said might seem quite obvious, but his words had a profound impact upon me and it's another important reality to be aware of:

*'It's not the **E**vent but how you **R**espond that determines the **O**utcome.'*

And then it hit me. For years I'd mistakenly believed that the reasons for the outcomes in my life had nothing to do with me, but were merely down to the events and circumstances I'd experienced. So when it came to my relationships with others, there had been times when I was responding to other people's behaviour by wearing the Victim T-Shirt (this is explained in Appendix A) – and not recognising that I had a choice in how I responded.

You're not Pavlov's dog

Ivan Pavlov (1849–1936) was a famous Russian scientist. He is perhaps best known for an experiment he conducted with dogs and which was rather originally called 'Pavlov's Dog Experiment'. From what I can gather (the experiments took place in the early part of the 20th century, so I'm not talking from first-hand experience), Ivan Pavlov noticed how much his dogs salivated when he was about to feed them. This gave him an idea. He decided to ring a bell just before he fed the dogs and to repeatedly do this over a period of days. Every time he rang the bell, he would then feed the dogs.

Then came the next part of his experiment. He decided to ring the bell and not feed the dogs. The bell rang. The dogs salivated. There was no food.

He repeated this over a period of days (some say he had a slightly cruel streak), ringing the bell and observing the dogs' reactions. Despite the fact that the dogs were never fed after the ringing of the bell, they continued to salivate (or dribble, as one of my delegates put it when describing the experiment to colleagues). The experiment helped Pavlov develop the theory of conditioned response. In this case, the bell was the stimulus and the saliva was the response.

So what has this got to do with your relationship with your boss, partner or children? Or your dog? Well, sometimes we behave in a way that closely resembles Ivan Pavlov's dogs. Let me explain. In our case, the stimulus might not be a bell, but perhaps a comment. For example:

- 'Have you put on weight?'

or

- 'Wanting to get in the boss's good books, eh?'

Or maybe it's to do with how people behave towards you. A supplier fails to return a call, a neighbour ignores you in the street or you open a door for someone and they fail to thank you.

All of the above are stimuli, or in Canfield's language, **E**vents. But unlike Pavlov's dogs, who became conditioned to respond in a certain way, we can **choose** how we respond. Obvious? Perhaps. But as I drove to work listening to the E + R = O concept being explained, I realised that up until that point, I'd failed to realise this important truth.

The work stuff

I was sharing the ideas of E + R = O with a group of sales managers. I asked them to tell me about an 'event' that invariably wound them up. The group of twelve (eleven men and one women) all identified the driving antics of other road users to be a major source of stress. In particular, the behaviour known as 'tailgaiting', whereby one driver deliberately drives extremely close to the car in front of them, in an attempt to force it to move over into a different lane, the assumption being that the car in front is driving too slowly and needs to make way. Their frustration came from the fact that this often occurred when they were driving in the fast lane and were driving at the speed limit. I asked how they tended to respond in such situations.

Just thinking about being tailgaited seemed to raise the energy levels in the room. The group's responses were animated.

- 'I brake when that happens.' (Now there's a mature, adult response.)
- 'Oh, I usually make a sign with my fingers that leaves them in no doubt what I think.' (This mature professional sales manager then demonstrated a couple of alternative 'hand signals', much to the group's roar of approving laughter.)

Being tailgaited was clearly not their favourite pastime. When it occurred, it demonstrated vividly how quickly road rage can develop. There was also a sense of, 'Well what else can we do? If a driver's being aggressive, we'll be aggressive back. We've no choice, have we?'

Then Linda spoke.

Like the rest of the group, as part of her job, Linda spent a great deal of time driving around the country meeting potential and existing clients.

'When a car tailgates me, I call it my chuckle time.'

The group looked bemused.

'Your chuckle time?'

'Yes, I've got this theory. Doesn't matter whether it's true or not, it works for me. Normally when a car drives aggressively close to my bumper, it's being driven by a man. And they're usually driving a big car. I've got a theory about men who drive big cars. So I quite happily move over and let them overtake me. But just as they're passing I take a very quick glance at them, chuckle and think – "small penis".' Several members of the group looked rather sheepish. I didn't because I felt affirmed in my manhood. I drive a Mini.

Linda experienced the same **e**vent as her colleagues but she made a different **r**esponse. Her **o**utcome was 'chuckle time': the rest of the group were close to road rage. It was a classic case of someone being able to manage their emotional response by reframing and re-interpreting the behaviour of someone else. Choosing to 'see' the event differently meant she 'responded' in a way that brought a much more satisfactory outcome.

SUMO pit stop

- What is it about other people's behaviour that 'winds you up' and makes you want to strangle them?

- Why do you think it winds you up so much?

- What's your usual response to this behaviour?

- What tends to be the outcome?

- How could you re-interpret the other person's behaviour so that you see it differently?

- On reflection, do you recognise that you do have a choice as to whether you 'handle' or 'strangle' so-called difficult people?

You've got the power

When we use phrases such as:

- 'They really wind me up';

- 'They bug me';

- 'I can't stand that person'; and

- 'My kids are really stressing me out'

We are in fact giving the control and power of how we respond to a situation to someone else. We're abdicating responsibility. Implied in our words is the following belief:

'**Your** behaviour determines **my** outcomes. I have no control over my response. I am a victim to your behaviour.'

> You're not a fish.
> You don't have to take the bait.

SUMO
wisdom

Can you relate to any of the phrases above? Don't beat yourself up if you can. The key to change starts with awareness. One of the keys to building better relationships is to recognise you need to take back control for how you respond to other people and also understand why you respond the way you do.

Andrew Matthews, author of the book *Making Friends*, sheds some light on what drives our response to certain people.

> Most times, when we get angry, it's not for the reasons we think. We get angry when we feel others don't care about us. We want respect. Everyone wants respect.

SUMO
wisdom

So why don't we always change how we respond?

Here are two reasons:

1 Handicapped by habit

Habits are powerful. They develop unconsciously over time, and take time and effort to change. For instance, do you find you have a quick temper? Well, it's perhaps unrealistic to expect to change suddenly overnight and to always respond in a more calm and appropriate way to situations. It's another reality we need to be aware of.

The following illustration will help you appreciate the power of habitual behaviour.

Imagine you're off for a walk in the countryside. You come to a field of tall grass. In fact, it's taller than you are (which,. in my case, is still not that tall). You know you need to get across the field, so you begin to move forward and clear a path through it. Eventually you get to the other side and continue your journey. The next day you come to the same field. What do 80 per cent of people tend to do – create a new pathway or choose the one they created yesterday? Eighty per cent of people will take the one they created yesterday. Why? It's easier. They know it will get them to where they want to go. It's safer, they know what to expect. It might not be the quickest or easiest route across the field, but it's the one they're most likely to take.

The above serves as a metaphor for how our brains work. Repeat a task over time, and the brain begins to establish a series of neural pathways. The more a particular task (or response to an event) occurs, the stronger the neural pathway. Decide to do something differently from how you've done it previously and it's like taking a new route across the field. Initially, this will be strange and perhaps even feel uncomfortable. To illustrate this further, when you're putting a jacket on, which sleeve do you put your arm into first? In my case, it's my right sleeve. Next time, try putting your other arm in the sleeve first. When I did this with my left arm it felt weird. I'd never done it before. I was creating a different neural pathway. But, if I continue to put my jacket on using my left arm first, it will eventually begin to feel more 'normal'. The same goes for developing a new habit or a different response. It might feel strange at first, but it is possible – your new response can become your 'normal' behaviour. You don't have to remain a permanent slave to your habits – but it can take time to change.

Shut Up being handicapped through habit.
Move On to choosing how to respond.

SUMO
wisdom

2 Mastered by motivation

One reason why we may decide not to change our response to events (or the actions of others) is because ultimately we suffer from the CIBA syndrome.

Can

I

Be

Ars*d?

The answer for some people is 'no'. We might talk about our decision to change, for example, 'I wish I didn't have such a short fuse'. But, ultimately, some people don't desire the change enough. It all comes down to a question of motivation. People that change are those that want to.

The personal stuff

Stewart, a delegate at one of my conferences, spoke about how he'd just got married and, as a part of the matrimonial package, he had acquired three step-sons. He confessed that, not having had children before, he found their behaviour (which was not out of the ordinary for three lads aged between eight and twelve) a challenge at times. He went on to elaborate.

'You see Paul, I've got quite a short temper. Only thing is, the lads still see their real father twice a week. I'd hate them to be reporting back to him, how I lose my temper, so I've really been working at keeping it under control. I don't want their father giving my wife grief if I lose it with the kids. I thought I'd got a short fuse, but I've been learning to lengthen it. It's not been easy, but it's working. Interestingly enough, I find I'm managing to control my emotions more effectively at work as well.'

Stewart was motivated enough to change his response. What about you?

SUMO pit stop

Identify a relationship that you would like to improve, either in or outside work:

- How are you currently responding to the other person's behaviour?

- What has been the outcome as a result of this response?

- How satisfied are you with the outcome?

- What's a realistic, improved outcome?

- On a scale of 1–10 (one is low, ten high) how motivated are you to choose a different response to create a different outcome?

- What needs to happen for you to increase that score?

- What are the consequences if you don't change your response?

It's worth remembering

In relation to how you're responding to other people, be aware of two of my 'Seven SUMO Questions'

1   Is my response appropriate and effective?

2   How can I influence or improve the situation?

Your SUMO takeaway

Events happen and people behave in some rather strange ways at times. Reality Rules. However the future of your relationships is not based upon a previous event – it's based upon how you respond to that event. Outcomes are not inevitable – they can be shaped and influenced by you. Take off the Victim T-shirt and take responsibility for how you're responding and engaging with others. Remember:

- You're not Pavlov's dog.

    Shut Up your previous conditioning.

    Move On to a new way of responding.

- You've got the power to change – but the people that change are the ones that want to.

- **Shut Up** being handicapped by habit.

    Move On to the freedom of new choices.

- **Shut Up** Can I Be Ars*d.

- **Move On** to finding a reason to change.

Wanting to strangle someone is a choice – so is learning how to handle them.

My SUMO Takeaway from 'E + R = O' is...

A Bit About the Beachball

Of all my six SUMO principles, 'Remember the Beachball' is perhaps the most relevant when it comes to relationships and it also builds upon our first two SUMO Realities 'Reality Rules' and 'E + R = O'.

For those of you who are sampling my SUMO ideas for the first time, let me elaborate on the beachball analogy. And for those of you who are already familiar with this principle, this chapter will act as a useful refresher as well as provide you with some new examples of how this idea works in practice.

The beachball explained

Imagine a large six-coloured beachball in the centre of the room. It is so large in fact, that it almost reaches the ceiling. Two groups of people are gathered, one on either side of the beachball. Ask one group the colour of the beachball and they answer, 'Red, white and blue'. The other people disagree. From where they're standing, it is actually coloured orange, green and yellow. Same beachball, different perspective. It's a simple analogy with important lessons. How we see the world (or beachball) can be very different to how others see it – but we can often act and communicate in a way that assumes that other people have the same perspective as ourselves. They don't. No matter how similar in outlook you are to another person, you will see some things differently. This isn't wrong, it's reality. And if I have a different perspective to you, I'm also likely to respond in a way you might not have expected.

> **SUMO wisdom**
>
> No matter how well you know a person — never assume you know everything that's going on in their world.

What influences people's perspectives?

In my first SUMO book, I focused on how our age, values, personality and current state of mind all influence our view of the world. Now I'd like to focus on what is one of the most important and, some would say, controversial factors that shapes our view of life.

Gender shapes our perspective

This is a big topic. (For a more in-depth exploration of the subject, look up the work of Allan and Barbara Pease who've written several books on the subject.) But let me explore briefly why many of our relationship challenges can be influenced by our gender. To put it bluntly, men and women can see very different sides of the beachball. The same event or experience may be interpreted very differently, as the following example illustrates:

Having spent Saturday night together, Tony and Cherie are asked to describe their perspective on how the evening went.

Cherie's side of the story

'He was in a strange mood when we met at the pub tonight. He was a lot quieter than normal. After a quick drink I suggested we take a taxi back to his place. As we drove back I told him that I loved him. And do you know what his reply was? Nothing. He put his arm around me but stared out of the window as he did so. What's that supposed to mean? He never tells me he loves me. Never. Anyway, when we got back to his place, we cuddled up on the sofa and watched some TV. I tried to get the conversation going but all I got from him was a couple of grunts. Typical. Well, the evening was going rapidly downhill, so I decided to go to bed. I'd had enough. After about ten minutes he joined me and we had sex. Then guess what? He fell asleep. I'm convinced this relationship is over. He's probably met someone else … any day now he's going to dump me. I just know he is. In the end I just cried myself to sleep.'

Tony's side of the story

'Tired. United lost. Had sex though.'

Stereotype or reality?

Whilst I do think stereotypes can be unhelpful and limiting, they sometimes contain a degree of truth. Stereotypes of certain nationalities may have no scientific basis, but when it comes to gender, there are a number of studies that do indicate some fundamental differences in how male and female brains operate. These differences can provide a powerful understanding of how men and women see the beachball differently and therefore provide some clues to the potential causes of conflict within male and female relationships.

The personal stuff

To be honest, I don't need any academic research to convince me that gender affects how we see and respond to life situations. How many examples do you want to illustrate the point? Here are a couple for starters.

Having travelled for over three hours from a conference I'd been speaking at, I arrived home ready for some chill time. I was not expecting conflict. My conversation with Helen, my wife, went something life this.

Me: Hi Babes.

Helen: Hi Hun. [I'd prefer Helen to call me 'Hunk' but her Mum always taught her to tell the truth.]

After a minute or two of silence whilst I go into the office and check emails and Helen eats the grapes I'd peeled for her earlier, the conversation continues.

Me: So what've you done today then?

Helen: I'll tell you what I've done. I've done the washing, the ironing, been shopping and finished the accounts. And what about you, Mr Perfect?

My harmless question had not quite elicited the response I'd expected. I thought (from a male perspective) that the question, 'So what have you done today then?' would be interpreted by Helen as a genuine request for information concerning her day. I thought she'd tell me about her day, ask me about mine and hey, after we'd connected on a verbal level, it may even lead to some intimacy in the bedroom. I got that one wrong.

Helen, judging by her response, heard words in my tone of voice that I'd never even said. She heard, 'So what've you done today … you lazy cow'.

Can I stress at this point that I have never called Helen a lazy cow, nor would I. But her reaction was such that I might as well have done. The research suggests women tend to be more sensitive (and I use that word in a positive context) to subtle changes in tone of voice than men are. My reality very much supports the research. Does yours?

Here Are A Few More Examples.

From my side of the beachball the words 'fine' and 'nice' are perfectly acceptable. Helen interprets them differently. So on the rare occasions that I do accompany Helen shopping, she will emerge from a changing room wearing a new item of clothing and ask me what I think. 'Yeah it's fine. It looks nice', I reply encouragingly. Such a response seems to generate waves of despair in Helen's mind. 'Fine? Nice? I'll leave it, let's try somewhere else.'

And when it comes to general conversation, is it just my perspective or do women feel the need to go into more detail than men?

When I ask a question, I'm usually after 'The News Headlines' approach, followed up by some detail if required. Some women I know seem much more keen to launch into a three-hour documentary about the events of the day. Now, is this the case with all men and women? No. Is it stereotyping men and women? Possibly. But is there some truth in it? Absolutely – based on my own experience and also the research I've studied.

Now for Helen's turn

So far, in terms of male and female relationships, you've only heard my male perspective. Now it's Helen's turn. So sit back and relax whilst Helen shares her view of the beachball. To do so, she addressed the following question:

Do you agree with Paul's view on the differences between men and women?

On the whole, yes, I do. I do think women are often better than men at interpreting what people mean when they communicate. Women are generally (but not always) better at observing people's body language, facial expressions and tone of voice. Therefore, when listening to people, women often subconsciously focus as much on the 'way' something is said as on the actual words that are said. This can be an invaluable skill, but we don't always get it right. I confess that I may read into a question something which is not there and, when I do, conflict or misunderstanding may arise. Paul and I often talk about 'intention' and 'impact'. Sometimes, his intention behind a comment is positive, but the impact is negative. Let me illustrate.

This year as Mothers Day approached, Paul and I experienced the same event but felt very differently. We went together to buy cards for our mums. We stood side by side in the card shop as we each chose a card. Paul remembered that he likes to get me a card on

Mothers Day (which is lovely) and decided to choose it whilst I was with him. But he doesn't quietly choose it and then hide it behind his mum's card, he tells me he's buying it now, so he doesn't have to come out to the shops again later. I hear this and interpret it very differently to the way Paul meant it.

I heard:

Helen I have forgotten to get you a card, it wasn't a priority and I can't be bothered to come out to the shops again just so it's a surprise for you.

Paul meant:

Helen I'm really sorry. I've not had a minute to get your card, but I really want to get you one now because I love you and you're a great mum.

Certainly the beachball principle has been invaluable for aiding our communication, although there have been times when I've been tempted to tell Paul where he can put his beachball!

SUMO pit stop

- If you have a close friendship with a member of the opposite sex, can you relate to any of the above examples?

- What has been your own experience?

- In what way have your gender differences impacted on your relationship?

More than two sides of the beachball

It's often tempting to see this principle as only being helpful when two people are interacting. Hopefully the following story illustrates its wider application.

I recently engaged in a rather challenging conversation with my son, Matt. It went something like this:

Matt: Dad, can I have a word?

Me: Sure Matt, fire away – as long as it's nothing to do with your maths homework.

Matt: [With the kind of face that says, 'Why on earth would I ever want to discuss that with someone who is as mathematically challenged as you?'] Dad, I don't support Bradford City any more. I prefer Wigan Athletic. They're my local team and next season they'll be in the Premiership. In fact, I'd like a Wigan shirt.

My response was unusual for me. I remained quiet. My brain was taking its time to process this act of treachery and betrayal. (It's at times like these that I'm glad counselling was invented.) OK, I'm being a little melodramatic, but it was a defining moment for me. (I'd beamed with pride just a couple of years previously when Matt was the mascot at Bradford City – it was a proud moment for me as he led the team onto the pitch.)

A week passed as I pondered on Matt's decision and then something remarkable happened. I decided to offer him the chance of a season ticket for Wigan – accompanied by me, of course. The draw of local Premiership football was too much to resist, even for me. I'd still make the trip across the Pennines to see Bradford when I could, but I was beginning to see the merits of travelling up the road to see the likes of Chelsea, Arsenal and Manchester United as opposed to Chesterfield, Bournemouth and Doncaster Rovers. There was just one stipulation: when Wigan were at home and, as we'd already paid for the tickets, I didn't want Matt to decide on a whim that the lure of going to a mate's house to play some bizarre computer game called 'The Lord of the Rings Meets Tomb Raider 58' would take precedence. He gave me his assurance.

As I write this I'm in Singapore, sitting outside Starbucks on Orchard Road. Tomorrow I present my first ever SUMO seminar in Asia. Yesterday, Wigan played their penultimate home game of the season against Aston Villa. Helen was taking Matt in my absence. I've just learned via text that Matt didn't go. He went to a mate's house for a sleepover. Helen let him. I think it's time to apply the Beachball principle.

My side of the beachball

- Matt and I had an agreement. He broke it.

- Sleepovers can happen anytime. Specific football matches can't.

- I wasted forty pounds to secure two empty seats.

- Helen, by allowing Matt to go to his sleepover, was being a soft touch. Helen didn't tell me they hadn't gone, Matt did.

I'll now hazard a guess as to how things look from Matt and Helen's perspective.

Matt's side of the beachball

- I really like my mate Tom and I've not been on a sleepover at his house before.

- It clashes with Wigan's game (only against Aston Villa), but Tom's away for the rest of the school holidays. It could be a while before the opportunity arises again.

- Mum might be able to take someone else.

- I was given a choice. I want to choose what I feel happiest about doing rather than go along to please someone else.

(Dad would call this taking responsibility for my actions rather than wearing the Victim T-Shirt.)

• Dad can afford it.

Helen's side of the beachball

• I'm up for the game – but I go because I enjoy these times with Matt, not because I'm an avid football fan.

• I know Paul will be disappointed if we don't go.

• Ruth has a friend coming over so taking her is not an option.

• I don't want Matt to go for my sake. If he's desperately keen to go to his mates, then that's his choice. I respect his decision. I'm glad he is able, in Paul's words, to 'communicate his needs'.

• It's an ordinary football match, not a cup final. It's Aston Villa not Manchester United. From my perspective, it barely registers a one on a scale of 1–10 in importance.

• I'm not soft, I'm a loving Mum who listens.

And the outcome? Wigan won. It was a cracking game. (They showed the goals in Singapore.) Sharing this example within an hour of discovering what happened is hugely helpful. It's helping me move on.

Shut Up seeing only one side to the story.
Move On to exploring other people's perspectives.

SUMO wisdom

SUMO pit stop

- If you were to apply what I've just done to your own relationship challenges, who would be the main people involved?

- Jot down their names below.

- What are their perspectives?

- Write down some key words to describe their view.

- What's influencing their view of the Beachball?

  - Person 1

  - Person 2

  - Person 3

- What thoughts have been triggered by doing this exercise?

- Do you need to take any actions as a result?

Your SUMO takeaway

- Our perspective on life is influenced by a whole bundle of factors. Reality rules – rarely will we view the world in exactly the same way as others do.

- How we 'see' things influences our response.

- **Shut Up** believing men and women are the same.

  Move On to recognising our unique differences.

- Remember that another person's perspective is valid for them – it's their reality.

- There are often several possible views of the same situation.

  Shut Up seeing the world only through your eyes.

  Move On to seeing things from other people's perspective.

- The beachball principle has maximum benefit in resolving relationship challenges when each party is prepared to embrace it.

Slow down your desire to strangle the other person – think about their perspective first.

My SUMO takeaway from 'A Bit About the Beachball' is ...

Stress Makes You Stupid

When it comes to relationships, I know the theory really well. I could write a book on it. (In case you hadn't noticed, you're reading it.) I also reckon I'm fairly self aware and every time I speak about my SUMO ideas, I get a chance to re-inforce them in my own mind. I work hard at 'walking my talk', but sometimes all my good intentions, knowledge and know-how flies out of the window ... when I enter the stress zone.

Stress is a reality for all of us. It influences how we respond to situations and is yet another factor in how we might view the beachball. Let's examine how the effects of stress can impact your relationships with others.

Myths about stress

First of all, let's get something straight about stress. If you have any books currently cluttering your shelves that preach 'You too can live a stress-free life', then do yourself a favour – bin them. 'Stress-free' is not achievable – in fact it's not even desirable.

We need pressure and stimulation to function as human beings. Imagine a limp elastic band. It's not doing what it was designed to do. It works when it's stretched, otherwise it's just useless. But there can be times when it's stretched too far and excessive stretching will weaken it. When this happens, it might snap. But an optimal state for an elastic band is not to be limp. The same goes for you and me. We were designed to have some 'stretch' in our lives. It's desirable to avoid excessive 'strain', but not to experience any degree of stress – or what I prefer to call 'healthy pressure' – can be equally unhealthy for us.

When stress makes you stupid

The average person has one brain. When you meet some people, you may question this fact, but it is true. However, your brain can trigger a reaction to an event or situation that could later cause you to look back with both regret and embarrassment. Although it's an extremely simplified illustration to describe the workings of such a complex and sophisticated piece of 'brain software', the following will explain why at times, we behave in the dumbest of ways. (Those of you who read SUMO may remember this illustration.)

If we take a cross-sectional view of your brain, we could divide it into three distinct sections:

1   **Rational brain** – sometimes referred to as the neo cortex or 'higher brain'. It is not yet fully formed when you are born.

2   **Emotional brain** – part of the limbic system. It is sometimes referred to as the 'mid brain'.

3   **Primitive brain** – also known as the reptilian brain or 'lower brain', it controls our 'fight or flight' response, our desire for food and our sex drive.

When work is steady, but not too busy, the customers are pleasant, the boss understanding and the children are well behaved, it's easy to respond in a rational way to most situations. A minor setback or the occasional 'difficult' customer can all be taken in your stride when you're in a relatively calm state.

But when you're tired, hungry, just dealt with the latest in a long line of challenging customers, recently heard about the latest proposed change at work, spent 40 minutes queuing in stationary traffic – then you're rapidly entering the strain zone. And your ability to rationalise and see things in perspective is quickly diminishing.

A child's untidy bedroom can seem much more of an issue now. The fact that your partner has once again left their toothbrush in the kitchen because they clean their teeth whilst walking around the house now registers a higher score on the 'stuff that irritates me' scale. (For more information on what inspired this example please read the chapter 'Develop Fruity Thinking' in my SUMO book.)

Here's the bottom line. When you're responding to a stressful situation, where your safety is on the line, primitive brain is a great place to be. In fact you wouldn't want to be any place else. You wouldn't want to spend time rationalising about the threat: 'I wonder if this man running towards me with a knife has a personal vendetta against me or is this just a random attack?' NO! You get into fight or flight mode. But what about when you're queuing in traffic and another motorist overtakes and pushes into the line ahead of you? Or you've just read your manager's appraisal of your performance at work over the last six months and their view contradicts your own? Primitive brain is now not a good place to be. The fight or flight response in this situation could lead to you saying or doing something that is completely inappropriate. Rational brain has been taken hostage and when primitive brain is in charge; common sense and a considered response are rarely to be seen

Shut Up reacting out of primitive brain.
Move On to engaging rational brain.

SUMO
wisdom

Let's get rational

My SUMO principle 'Develop Fruity Thinking' explores how to use what psychologists refer to as a cognitive behavioural approach to moving out of primitive brain into rational brain. I developed seven questions which can be useful to ask yourself in certain situations. I'll mention them briefly here – they are also in Appendix B.

1   Where is this issue on a scale of 1–10 (where 10 = death)?

2   How important will this be in six months' time?

3   Is my response appropriate and effective?

4   How can I influence or improve the situation?

5   What can I learn from this?

6   What will I do differently next time?

7   What can I find that's positive in this situation?

(You can download these questions for free by going to www. TheSumoGuy.com and clicking on 'free stuff'.)

These are great questions to use when you feel you're in the strain zone. And they reinforce the insight E + R = O (**E**vent + **R**esponse = **O**utcome). By asking yourself one of these questions, it can influence both your perspective and response to a situation. Your relationship with a friend, colleague, customer or partner could benefit by reflecting on one of these questions. But don't take my word for it – read Caroline's story.

The personal stuff

Caroline was a delegate on one of my workshops. She'd lived with her boyfriend for two years and, although 'in love', she did find herself over-reacting to one or two of his habits. One of these habits seems to be shared by men throughout the world. In fact, I wonder if when boys are very young (and perhaps too young to remember) our fathers take us to one side and say 'Son, one day you'll be a man. There are many things that will mark you out as a man, but one above all that will define you as a real man. Follow this rule, my son, and you will indeed embrace manhood:

'Never ever under any circumstances put the toilet seat down when you've finished.'

Now I understand this is a minor irritation for some women, but not for our Caroline. Minor irritation? You've got to be kidding. Despite numerous requests on her part, Steve continued to adhere to the ancient male ritual of leaving the toilet seat up. What did Caroline do? Well, her primitive brain took over – she stormed out of the bathroom (she didn't make clear what state of undress she was in at the time, but if you use your imagination it does make the illustration even more hilarious), stormed down stairs, grabbed the remote control (which judging by men's attachment to such a device, must evoke memories of breastfeeding or being in the womb) and promptly marched Steve back into the bathroom. The conversation went something like this:

Caroline: Just how many times do I have to tell you?

Steve: Tell me what?

Caroline: Tell you about the bloody toilet seat.

Steve: What's wrong with it?

Caroline: It's up.

Steve: And?

Caroline: It should be down. The toilet seat should be down.

Steve: Well if it's such a big deal, why don't you just put it down?

Caroline: I shouldn't have to. Anyway, how would you like it if I poured my cigarette ash onto your head?

Steve: What's that got to do with the toilet seat?

Caroline: Everything. It's just another way in which you fail to show me any respect or consideration.

All was not well with Caroline and Steve, but then Caroline attended a Customer Service workshop I was running for her company. Having heard some of my SUMO principles she began to realise an important truth.

SUMO wisdom

One of the single biggest causes of stress in your life is ... yourself.

The insight E + R = O suddenly made sense to Caroline. 'It's not the position of the toilet seat that counts, but how I respond.' In recounting her story, Caroline explained that two of my SUMO questions had dramatically influenced her response to the 'bathroom issue'.

1   Where is this issue on a scale of 1–10 (where 10 = death)? and

2   How important will this be in 6 months' time?

Steve can now rest secure that if he does unintentionally forget to put the toilet seat down, he and his remote control will come to no harm. Caroline still needs to remind him occasionally with 'a quiet word in his ear', but generally she now feels less stressed about what is, in the grand scheme of things, a fairly trivial issue.

SUMO pit stop

What trivial issues or irritating habits of others are you allowing to cause you stress at the moment?

Why Hippo Time is helpful

What do hippos do in mud? Yes, besides break wind and empty their bowels. You got it – they wallow. 'Hippo time is OK' is one of my main SUMO principles and can be particularly helpful during times of upset, setback and frustration. (In fact I'm hoping that the Bradford City Chairman, having read this book, names a section of the ground 'The Hippo Stand'.) However, I want to suggest that it's because people don't have enough Hippo Time that they end up being so stressed. This then has a knock on effect on our relationships with others. You see, Hippo Time isn't just about a place to wallow. Hippos also go into mud or water in order to cool down and get out of the heat. And I wonder how many times we overreact to a comment or a situation because we're overheated? Are you feeling so stressed that you do feel you could literally strangle someone?

So how can you prevent yourself getting overheated in the first place? What practical strategies can you take when you recognise, 'I need some Hippo Time in order to cool down and alleviate some stress'?

Here are five ideas to help

- **Let's do lunch.** During a busy day at work we may often believe, 'I haven't time for lunch.' Well, you may not have time for a leisurely hour's break, but do take some time out for yourself. Go for a short walk, read a paper, do the crossword. Whatever you do, disengage your brain from what you've been doing. Have a brain break and give yourself time to cool down from the heat of your earlier activity. Doing so will actually make you more productive later in the day. Whilst your conscious brain is focused on what type of coffee to purchase (in some places, this could be as many as 44 different options), your subconscious brain has an opportunity to deal with some of the issues of the morning. Your 'time out' could trigger a flash of inspiration later in the day and help you deal more calmly with that difficult colleague or customer.

- **Sweat it out**. By now you'll have realised that I'm a great believer in trying to rationalise and think through solutions to particular challenges you're faced with. But sometimes I decide to do a 'thinking bypass operation' and immerse myself in some form of physical activity. If I want to give my best in my relationships at work and at home, I need to recognise the importance of exercise. For starters, exercise increases 'alpha waves' – electrical brain patterns associated with being calm. It can also help achieve the following:

  - lower blood pressure;
  - improve the quality of your sleep;
  - raise the levels of endorphins (chemicals in your brain that can give you feelings of wellbeing and contentment); and
  - raise your self esteem.

Pretty good, eh? But, more importantly, these benefits can indirectly affect how we deal and respond to people in our lives. That irate customer may seem less of a challenge because, physically and psychologically, you're in a better state to deal with them. And your kid's untidy bedroom may not warrant such an outburst if you've already expended some of your energy (and perhaps frustration) in a more worthwhile direction.

SUMO
wisdom

Shut Up slobbing about.
Move On to sweating it out.

Exercise doesn't necessarily equate to going to the gym. Find something (or perhaps discover something) you enjoy doing which requires some physical exertion. For instance, helpful Hippo Time for some people may mean starting a dance class – although hopefully you'll move with a little more grace and style than a hippo.

- **Have a Laugh.** The Book of Proverbs, which was written before I was a lad, claims that laughter really is the best medicine. It seems some of the ancient writers from the past had a point. Scientists at Waterloo University in Ontario recently established that exposure to humour improves immune system function, producing significant rises in the body's natural defences such as antibodies in the bloodstream. Perhaps at times, the biggest source of laughter comes when we take a step back and look at ourselves.

Sometimes we take ourselves and our problems too seriously. Learning to laugh at yourself is both helpful and healthy.

SUMO
wisdom

- **Muse to the music.** Difficult day ahead? Aware that the only noise you're currently hearing is the sound of your own strained voice screeching various commands to those around you? Reach for your iPod or whatever other music system you have and unwind to your favourite sounds. It doesn't have to be calming music (although this may help) but, if it makes you feel good, make sure your Hippo Time is tuneful.

- **Remember the sound of silence.** Maybe it's not the music you need to listen to, but some silence. Life in the 21st century can be a constant bombardment of noise. Create some silence in your life. Go for a walk. Enjoy your own company. Experience the sounds of nature. Perhaps this is not necessarily a time to think – but simply a time to be.

For more tips on how to deal with stress, go to www.TheSumo-Guy.com and click on 'free stuff'.

The work stuff

Helen is a great support to me in managing the business, but ultimately I'm responsible for winning new work and delivering the goods. After a speaking engagement I may have a long journey home. By the time

I arrive back, I am not only greeted by my wife (unless she's watching a medical drama on TV, in which case I'm greeted with the phrase, 'Hi love, if you're making a drink, mine's a tea') but also by a stack of emails and other messages.

My office is at home. It's convenient. It's also a challenge. It's easy to work late and start early. By 9am it can be satisfying to have completed nearly three hours' work, but it can also be draining if I don't build in some 'recovery time' during the day.

However, my biggest challenge is guilt. There's always something to do. Yet, for my own sanity and for the benefit of my relationships with others, Hippo Time is a necessity. For me this does not necessarily constitute doing nothing, but doing something different.

What revitalises and refreshes me?

Some of it is fairly mundane: reading the paper; having a cappuccino in my favourite café; watching football on TV; going for a walk by the canal; or sending a text message to a friend. These are not optional extras if I find the time – they are necessities. Without them, I'll be in the stress zone and I can say from experience that stress can make you stupid. So when I find I'm becoming increasingly irritated by people in general, then I know that it's my body's way of saying, 'We need to plan some Hippo Time – we need to get out of the heat, cool down and play.'

SUMO pit stop

- In what ways does stress affect your relationships with others?

- Which one of the seven SUMO questions do you want to be particularly conscious of using more in the future?

- What are you doing for you? What refreshes and revitalises you? What helps you switch off?

When you are low on energy, you're also low on patience and tolerance.

SUMO wisdom

SUMO takeaway

S.U.M.O. TAKEAWAY

How I interact and engage with other people will be influenced by my emotional state. Feeling tired, frustrated and off balance will hinder my ability to connect positively with others.

When I'm stressed:

- I won't think rationally;

- I won't see things in perspective;

- Trivial issues will seem like major problems;

- I won't be much fun to live or work with;

- I will overreact to situations;

- I will be damaging my health; and

- I will feel like strangling someone.

In order to Shut Up, Move On from stress, I need to remember:

- To get rational and 'Develop Fruity Thinking'; and

- that Hippo Time is helpful and may include:

  - *Lets do lunch* – taking a break from work sometime during the day;
  - *Sweat it out* – take some exercise;
  - *Have a laugh* … particularly at yourself;
  - *Muse to the music*; and
  - *Remember the sound of silence.*

My SUMO takeaway from 'Stress Makes You Stupid' is …

Investment Pays

Since being a teenager, I have struggled to keep my weight under control. If you've met me, you might be slightly surprised at that statement, particularly if I had my clothes on at the time (and I guess on most occasions I would!). I suppose I'm in relatively good shape for my age, but I work hard to achieve this. Since I recovered from being ill with Chronic Fatigue Syndrome, there have been very few weeks where I haven't taken some form of exercise and, when I don't, the weight is quick to reappear.

How I wish I had the metabolism of my brother. He has no such worries (and he's several inches taller and much better looking than me ... but, hey, I'm not bitter).

What victories I've achieved in the weight department have taken time and they continue to take time. There's no quick fix to maintaining my fitness, it stems purely from such exciting words as 'discipline' and 'consistency'.

Building better relationships with others is just the same. No matter how good the course or seminar on how to improve your relationships is, it's what you do on a daily basis that counts. Reading this book will provide you with plenty of ideas and insights. It may even give you some inspiration and motivation. But it can't force you to take action. If you want better relationships, *you* have to do something. You have to invest time, commitment and energy.

Let's examine two insights that shed some light on why relationships – both in and outside the workplace – can often break down or drift apart due to a lack of investment.

> **SUMO wisdom**
>
> *Great relationships don't magically happen. They stem from the process of continually making positive choices.*

Meaningless motivation

Some managers believe that 'once-a-year praise' is enough to sustain the morale and motivation of their staff for the next twelve months. I call such an attitude 'meaningless motivation'. Let me elaborate.

When I'm away working, I invariably stay in hotels. I enjoy doing this most of the year – except during December. You see, in December, whilst I'm at the hotel on my own (unless I've tracked down a Bradford City fan who now lives in the area), the rest of the place is thronging with people on their staff Christmas party. Sometimes there's a separate corner of the restaurant sectioned off for residents of the hotel who are not involved in the party. As I'm escorted to the table by my waiter or waitress, I can sense they're thinking, 'This is the saddo's section, Sir. We reserve this area for people like yourself who have no mates.' Occasionally I hover close to the function room and look in at what I'm missing. On one occasion, the group had just finished their meal and the owner or managing director stood to address the hundred or so staff, most of whom were wearing party hats.

'Well, it's been a difficult year, but I'd just like to say how much I've appreciated all your hard work.'

At that point of his talk I looked at the people he was addressing. Silence. No smiles. No one nodded in acknowledgement at what was being said. Some seemed more interested in topping up their coffee cups or fighting over the remaining mint chocolate. Others were more interested in the Christmas decorations. Whatever their 'leader' was saying to them didn't appear to be having the desired impact. Perhaps I'm making a massive assumption, but I sensed it would be next Christmas before they were told again how valued they were. He quickly sat down. The disco began. The energy returned.

The incident got me thinking. It seems, for some managers, that Christmas is the only time of year they think about thanking their staff. It's a bit like going to the gym once a year and declaring, 'I try to keep fit.' Don't get me wrong – I'm not against Christmas parties – even when I am the only person in the hotel not attending one. But I am against managers believing that one-off motivational speec h will sustain staff morale until the next annual get-together.

Meaningless motivation is not just restricted to the workplace. I think we can also fall into the same trap in our personal lives.

For instance, some parents seem to rarely have time for their children, but think that buying them a massive birthday or Christmas present will help magically create a meaningful relationship. It doesn't. And waiting for an anniversary before you express any sign of gratitude to your partner is equally devoid of any real long-term benefit.

SUMO pit stop

- If you're a manager, when did you last invest some time in having a meaningful one-to-one conversation with members of your team?

- In your personal life, when did you last invest some time having a meaningful one-to-one conversation with someone close to you?

- When did you last show appreciation and gratitude to a loved one?

> **SUMO wisdom**

What you invest in grows.

Here's the second reason as to why relationships breakdown or drift apart:

Beware the boiled frog syndrome

Most of us are very busy. The phrase often used to describe Western society is 'cash rich, time poor'. Living life this way is killing relationships. Yet the challenge for many of us is to actually recognise and be aware of how many relationships can be damaged due to the lack of time we invest with each other. 'OK,' you say, 'I get your point, but what has this got to do with boiled frogs?' Good question. Let me explain.

Firstly, may I clarify that I've never tried this, but apparently, if you place a live frog in a pan of boiling water it jumps out immediately. No surprise there. However, place a frog in a pan of lukewarm water however and it will swim around quite happily. You can then, if you are so inclined, gradually begin to heat up the water. I understand by taking this approach, it's possible for the water to reach such a temperature that the frog suddenly finds itself being boiled alive. (If you're reading this whilst eating something I do apologise.) The frog's death is caused by the gradual, not the dramatic, change in its environment.

That's what can happen in relationships. Although there can be occasions when something sudden and dramatic happens that damages the relationship, more often than not, people simply drift apart.

Now this may sound like I'm talking solely about relationships outside of work, but I'm not. Managers can drift apart from their staff. Initially, new starters are welcomed with open arms. There are regular reviews and feedback on progress. Then, over time, this starts to happen less. Perhaps understandably so. But if this goes unchecked, staffs' sole opportunity for some meaningful dialogue happens only at the dreaded annual appraisal.

Silence isn't always golden. Sometimes silence sends the message, 'I take you for granted.'

SUMO wisdom

So how can you avoid this relationship drift or breakdown? What practical steps can you take to ensure you invest time with some of the key people in your life? Here's a couple of ideas to consider.

Make a date

Finding time to have meaningful conversation with a colleague or your partner can, I admit, be a challenge. But read the following slowly and allow the words to sink in. A LACK OF TIME IS NO EXCUSE.

I always make time for things that are important. If you recognise more time with certain key people in your life is necessary, then quit wearing the victim T-shirt and bleating, 'But I can't find the time.' Make time. 'I haven't got the time' really means, 'I'm prioritising something else that means more to me.'

Your relationships with other people are critical to your emotional wellbeing and personal success. If you choose not to make the time, then be prepared to live with the consequences. The Relationship Foundation in Cambridge talks about 'Relationship Pensions' – the idea being that we need to invest in relationships now if we want to have them in the future.

Some people's relationship fund is in serious need of fresh investment.

SUMO wisdom

The work stuff

Tony is a director of a small caravan company in Scotland. I did some work for them recently. We went out for dinner together and he talked about how difficult it was to motivate his staff.

'How well do you know them?' I asked.

'What do you mean?' he replied.

'How well do you know them as people? What are their personal circumstances? What are their dreams? What's their history?'

'I can't ask them all those questions', Tony said.

'No, I realise you can't and certainly not out of the blue at the coffee break. But at least try and find out a little more about them as people and how they're finding work.'

Tony took up my challenge. Rather than hide away in his office every day at lunch with his head buried in the paper, he decided to spend at least one lunch time every week with one or two members of staff. They chatted mainly about cars and football, but then one of them admitted he felt under pressure at home as he and his partner were struggling to start a family. Tony is convinced he'd never have found this out unless he'd suggested they go for lunch. Over the next few months, Tony asked very casually but sincerely, 'How are things at home?' He also added, 'You know where I am if you need me.'

Tony's conclusion to all this? He felt more aware that his staff are not simply workers, but people. He recognised there were dangers to this more personal approach, but thought it was worthwhile. 'I don't want to get too close to my staff because I feel that is unhealthy. Neither do I want to be a counselling service. But I sense some of the team are a little more committed to the organisation because I was prepared to take some time out for them.' How much time did Tony invest in this? About four hours a month.

Not everyone likes to open up and talk about their personal lives. That's fine. That's not your goal. The aim is to simply create opportunities and space for people to talk about whatever is on their mind. A great way to facilitate this is often over some food and drink. Choose a relaxed environment, switch off your phone and go without an agenda and above all go there with an attitude of wanting to listen.

Something is clearly wrong if the point a manager discovers a colleague is unhappy at work is when they hand in their notice.

SUMO wisdom

The personal stuff

I once read that kids spell the word 'love' T I M E. I felt uncomfortable when I read that. My work takes me away from home a lot. It's the nature of my business. Reality rules. But I realised that if I didn't make time for Matt and Ruth when they were younger – then they won't have time for me when I'm older. Here's what I've been attempting to do. When the kids were at the same school I would purposely do all I could to avoid working on a Friday afternoon. It wasn't always possible, but because I made it my goal, it happened a lot more than if I'd simply left it to chance. We would go to the Green Door Café. We ordered the same thing every time. It became a ritual. It's Friday, it's The Green Door. We were probably only in there 40 minutes. The kids sometimes argued, I told them off, we laughed, we talked, we played a game involving trying to hit each others hands. They got a lolly from Karen, the owner and we tried to avoid the cracks on the paving stones as we walked back to the car. Not particularly exciting, but I loved it. Writing about it now conjures up almost the same emotions as when Bradford City win a corner. I guess the whole experience only took up an hour each Friday, but I hope that when Dad departs from this planet, Matt and Ruth will remember 'The Green Door Days'.

Rituals and routines can reinforce relationships.

SUMO wisdom

Remember your stars (and the people closest to you)

Some staff are good workers – some are even stars. They work hard. They do a great job. The customers love them. Our mistake? We take them for granted.

Some staff are difficult. They do the minimum required. They provide barely acceptable service to the customer. We spend time with them. Their lack of performance demands our attention.

Star performers that are taken for granted will not maintain their level of commitment and enthusiasm indefinitely. Like organisations that do so much to attract new customers yet ignore the needs of their existing ones, so resentment begins to develop amongst stars who are ignored.

Eventually you're faced with a member of the team who's no longer performing to their previously high levels and it's only then that they're actually 'noticed'.

The same can be true in our personal lives. We can mistake close physical proximity for intimacy. Because we see those closest to us regularly, we can fail to see the need for investing meaningful time with each other. The reality can be that we direct our emotional energy elsewhere and neglect the needs of those closest to us.

SUMO pit stop

- Who in your life do you need to spend some quality time with?

- If you were to take one action today to ensure you had quality time with this person, what would it be? Why don't you take a break from reading this book and take some action now?

Everybody wears an invisible sign around their neck: 'Please notice me and make me feel important.
p.s. There are consequences to ignoring this sign.'

> **SUMO wisdom**

The personal stuff

If you've read my previous book, you'll know that 1997 was an interesting year for me. Lots of international travel, lots of business ... and lots of stress. I rarely said 'no' to any work request, and if a friend wanted advice, I was always on hand. On reflection the only people I was saying 'no' to were my family. By rarely being available, I was saying 'no' to their requests for time and attention. To go back to a previous analogy, if we're talking frogs in water, then the temperature was rising rapidly, but I was too busy to even notice. It was only when Helen pointed out my huge blind spot and the impact my behaviour was having on her and the kids that I finally got the message. No one was permanently scarred, but it took a while for the wounds to heal.

Recently though, the wounds were re-opened as I once again slipped into a similar pattern of behaviour. I still find life a challenge, stress is rarely far from me and I struggle on occasions to recognise my own limitations. As I work with a passion to help others, I'm reminded of the phrase 'Physician heal thyself'. Helen and I have needed to talk about our relationship. I sensed I'd been operating on cruise control and wasn't being pro-active in how I invested my time with her. I'd like to say our conversations were easy – they weren't. But we chose not to ignore our problem or allow it to escalate – we chose to do something about it. Perhaps it's only over time that you begin to notice the impact of your investment and whether or not your relationship fund is in need of some 'topping up'.

The grass is always greener where it's watered.

> **SUMO wisdom**

Your SUMO takeaway

- Successful relationships at home or work don't magically happen – they take time. Usually, the larger the investment, the greater the reward.

- If things have been going wrong over the last few years, do not expect them to be resolved within a few days.

- *Beware meaningless motivation.* A one-off 'thank you' does not compensate for ongoing support and appreciation.

- *Beware the boiled frog syndrome.* Relationship challenges can creep up on us almost unnoticed.

- *Make a date.* Be proactive in planning time with others.

- *Remember your stars and the people closest to you.* Avoid the trap of taking people for granted.

SUMO wisdom

Shut Up drifting along to relationship oblivion.
Move On to investing in a better relationship.

My SUMO takeaway from 'Investment Pays' is ...

Give Yourself the VIP Treatment

In the previous SUMO Reality, we explored why 'Investment Pays'. In this SUMO Reality, our focus is on why we need to specifically invest in our relationship with ourselves. If 'Stress Makes You Stupid' focused on how external factors affect our ability to relate and connect with others, then this reality reveals the impact of what's happening internally with ourselves.

Two thousand years ago, a Jewish Carpenter who based himself in the area now known as Palestine spent the last three years of his life speaking to people about issues to do with life and death. His thoughts and ideas have influenced and inspired billions of people around the world and whatever your view of this man, you'll have to admit, he said some pretty profound things. I like his style. He loved to tell stories, challenge people's current way of thinking and he kept things simple. I guess in many ways he's become my role model. One of his messages was this:

'Love your neighbour as yourself.'

Five words. So much insight. I'm no theologian, but I think a whole book could be dedicated to that short statement. Here's the angle I'd like to take. It's not as succinct, but I admit that I'm not in the Carpenter's league.

'If you want to build better relationships with others, learn to build a better one with yourself.'

It's your thoughts that count

A key SUMO truth is this – how people think affects the quality of their lives. In my previous SUMO book I explored the **TEAR** model which is explained in more detail in Appendix A. Here's how the model works:

What I **T**hink about 'me' can affect how I feel (**E**motions) about 'you'. This influences how I **A**ct (or behave) towards you, and over time my actions will produce certain outcomes or **R**esults in our relationship.

Let's expand on this further.

Insecure or steady and stable?

Most people will admit to times in their lives when they felt insecure. I certainly have. Feelings of insecurity can have many causes; we may be struggling with our personal identity, our self-image or our self-esteem. Perhaps some setback has led us to believe not simply that we've 'failed', but more significantly – 'I am a failure'. Feelings of self-worth can fall dramatically and we can view the success of others in a negative way. In fact, other people's achievements only serve to reinforce our feelings of failure. In such a state, it's difficult to reach out in a positive and meaningful way to other people. Our perception of others is seen through the glasses of low self-esteem. Our view can be distorted. We may interpret people's behaviour as arrogant and brash, rather than as confidence. And even if our perception of how people behave is accurate, we may struggle to deal with them effectively because of how we see ourselves. A poor self image can give rise to both passive and aggressive responses.

	My view of me	**My view of you**
Passive Response	I'm not OK	You're OK

This way of thinking believes that my needs are not as important as yours. Therefore I often fail to communicate what I need; or to make my own feelings known. My response to conflict could be to wear the Victim T-shirt and, because I don't feel great about me, I allow others to take advantage. I see my desires as secondary to others and I fail to appreciate my own value or worth. The reality is my relationships are not based on equality or mutual respect.

And the consequences?

I may allow myself to be bullied by my boss, be constantly put down by my partner or manipulated by my children. Outwardly I respond in a passive manner – but inwardly, bitterness and resentment begin to take root. A vicious cycle of behaviour develops and I can be deluded into thinking the problem is with the other person – when in fact the problem stems from how I see myself.

	My view of me	**My view of you**
Aggressive Response	I'm not OK	You're not OK

In this context the problem remains the same, but how I deal with not being OK about me is expressed differently. As I lack strategies to raise my own self-esteem and self-worth, I compensate by dragging you down. In this response I use aggressive behaviour as a way of controlling others. If I can make you feel weak, then that helps me to feel strong – at least temporarily. My sense of worth is fuelled by your sign of weakness.

(There can of course be other reasons for aggressive behaviour – alcohol is probably the main one, but inappropriate role models or feeling stressed can also trigger an aggressive reaction.)

SUMO pit stop

- How would you describe your relationship with yourself?

- Could the cause of a relationship challenge you have at present be linked to how you currently view yourself?

How to be OK with yourself

I'm not a huge animal lover, unless you can call owning two goldfish a sign of being one. (Since first writing this, we've now acquired two cats, but more of that later.) However, if you gave me a thoroughbred horse or a pedigree dog, I'd know how to look after them. I would make sure they had regular exercise, were well groomed and that they ate well. I wouldn't let either animal 'do its own thing' in terms of diet and exercise. I wouldn't coop them up all day and feed them my leftover scraps. I'd take their care seriously. Yet I have to confess that my attitude towards myself – my health and looking after my own needs – doesn't always evoke the same caring response as I might give to a couple of animals. On reflection, I think that's quite bizarre – don't you?

SUMO wisdom

My gift to you is a healthy me.

Let's wake up to the fact – you need to take responsibility for a 'healthy, OK you'. And here are four ways to be OK with yourself.

1 Accept the positives about you

Let me remind you (for those of you already familiar with my SUMO book) of an incredibly important quote:

The most important person you will ever talk to is yourself.

Let me spend an hour with you and I'll begin to get an idea of what you think about yourself. Your words might not tell me everything, but they will provide me with sufficient clues.

When I give people a compliment, a two-word response, 'Thank you', will usually indicate a healthy self-image. I rarely hear those two words.

> When someone gives you a compliment, it may contradict the view you have of yourself.

SUMO wisdom

I appreciate some compliments are not given sincerely, but those that are, are gifts. It would be rude not to accept a gift, but many of us refuse to receive them when they're in the form of praise or positive feedback. Why? Embarrassed? Feeling uncomfortable for some reason? Perhaps you're not used to receiving them. Next time you receive a compliment, pause and take a moment to receive it – and then thank the other person for it.

The personal stuff

I was working on a project about developing the idea of 'SUMO for kids'.

Gill, who's helping me with this idea is also a friend. She's a talented woman. There's a lot I admire and respect about her and I believe it's important to let her know that. (I'm not going to wait for her funeral to say nice things about her.) However I noticed that one particular conversation went something like this:

Me: That was a good meeting today, I really appreciated your help.

Gill: When's the next one?

Me: Well we still need to arrange it. I just hope the others are as focused as you are. You had some excellent ideas today and I felt inspired. I really appreciate all you're doing on this project.

Gill: Will we meet at the same hotel or go for a different venue next time?

Here's my point. Not only was Gill not receiving my 'gift' but her response wasn't doing a great deal for me either. I guess the Jewish

Carpenter who we spoke about earlier hit the nail on the head (do those last six words secure my nomination for the worst pun of the year?) when he said, 'It's more blessed to give than to receive.' Now I'm not quite sure what he meant by 'blessed' but I do know I get a real buzz out of doing something which clearly makes the other person feel good. Gill, by not accepting or even acknowledging my thanks, didn't actually make me feel good. I felt my gift had been ignored. We talked about it. We resolved the issue. She gave me permission to use this illustration and she's learning to accept compliments.

SUMO wisdom

Shut Up refusing the gift of positive feedback. Move On to receiving it with thanks.

Another way to be OK with yourself …

2 Shut up the Inner Critic, listen to the Inner Coach

I've explored this idea further in the SUMO principle 'Develop Fruity Thinking' in my previous SUMO book – but here's a brief overview. The Inner Critic – the voice inside your head that highlights your weaknesses and undermines your confidence – may convince you that you're not worthy of positive feedback or, worse still, that by accepting it, you're one step away from being the most arrogant person on the planet.

Your Inner Coach is the complete opposite. Although it is prepared to challenge you, it also knows how to care for you. The Coach knows that positive feedback can help build your confidence and feelings of self-worth whilst the Critic is keen to condemn and make you feel worthless. When you make a mistake, the Critic welcomes the opportunity to stage an internal boxing match – where the only opponent is you. When the Critic takes centre stage in your life, your ability to engage positively with others is drastically reduced. You're likely to use language that puts yourself down and be in a frame of mind that finds it difficult to say positive things about others. It's hardly a recipe for a healthy relationship.

> Next time you find your Inner Critic condemning you, ask yourself, what would my Inner Coach say to me at this point?

SUMO wisdom

Paradoxically, one possible consequence of listening too much to the Inner Critic is that when we're around others we feel the need to overcompensate. If I'm OK with me, then I'm happy to give other people space and time to talk about themselves. But when I'm not OK about me, then I may feel the need to dominate the conversation and overcome my feelings of inadequacy by trying to impress everyone I meet.

So what does the Coach do? The Coach identifies your strengths as well as your weaknesses. The Coach's desire is to build upon your strengths (it's a false belief that strengths take care of themselves) and help you manage with your weaknesses. The Critic is keen for you to ignore your strengths and simply focus (as opposed to work on) your weaknesses. The Inner Critic often addresses you in the third person and uses phrases such as:

- 'You'll never be able to …';

- 'You're awful/hopeless at …';

and sometimes in the first person

- 'I'll never be able to …'; and

- 'I'm hopeless at …'

> When you dwell on a failure or a setback you drain yourself of self-belief and confidence.

SUMO wisdom

So how does the Inner Coach communicate to you? The tone of voice you hear inside your head is more supportive and encouraging. When you've had a setback, the Inner Coach asks questions such as:

- 'Where is this issue on a scale of 1–10 (where 10 equals death)?'

- 'How can I influence or improve the situation?'

- 'What can I learn from this?'

- 'What will I do differently next time?'

The Coach also gets you to focus on positives:

- 'What went well today?'

- 'What do I like about me?'

These are great questions to help build up your confidence and enable you to focus on solutions rather than just problems.

SUMO wisdom

If you want to build a healthy relationship with others, start cultivating a long-term relationship with your Inner Coach. You've probably spent years entertaining your Inner Critic. The relationship is going nowhere — it's time to finish it.

Another way to be OK with yourself ...

3 Postpone permanently pleasing people

A hotel I was staying at had staff wearing the following badge:

We never say no.

Well it certainly raised my expectations about the service I would receive – until, that is, a duty manager (who'd clearly not bought into the philosophy) remarked, 'Well, we've just become skilled in saying 'no' in a different way'.

So what's my point? Some people can be so driven in their desire to please others that they might as well wear a badge that states:

I never say no.

So why say no?

Our desire to continually say 'yes' to others ultimately stems from our desire to be liked and accepted. Our rationale can be, 'If I say no, I will disappoint the other person and they will no longer approve of me.' It's a fundamental human need to be loved and accepted by others. But constantly striving to find this acceptance can be unhealthy. If my belief is that I'm only OK when others tell me I'm OK, then I become a prisoner to other people's opinions. For you and me to function as healthy human beings, psychologically and emotionally, we need to develop a positive regard for ourselves that is not solely based upon the views of other people. When you're less reliant on external approval, you become less of a people pleaser and are more comfortable saying 'no' to the requests of others.

'I don't know the key to success but I know the key to failure — trying to please everyone.'
Bill Cosby

SUMO wisdom

The personal stuff

When my first SUMO book was published, I relied a little too heavily on the opinion of others to influence how I personally felt about it. I tended to feel positive only when others made positive comments.

One close friend remarked how she'd enjoyed my previous book on stress more. A harmless remark. She wasn't saying she hadn't enjoyed this book. But after a particularly busy schedule I was physically and emotionally drained. For a brief time I felt unable to access my own internal reference points about what I thought about my work. My emotions fluctuated based purely upon the comments of other people.

Fortunately for me, I began to receive emails from strangers praising the book and the initial sales were extremely healthy. But it wasn't a good place to be. Relying solely on the views of others to determine your own self-worth never is.

Gradually through the wise counsel of friends – particularly John, Molly and Jeanie – I began to get perspective. They each gently pointed out how I had become overdependant on external approval in their own way.

Their message ultimately was, 'Paul, whatever people think about your book, you're an OK person'.

Then Jeanie asked me a direct question, 'What do *you* think about the book?' I realised that, although we all need some external feedback and approval, we also need to develop a strong internal sense of accepting ourselves. Then it dawned on me – I was actually quite proud of my book.

It is possible to go to the other extreme however. Some people choose to completely ignore the opinions and feedback of others. My friend Dave, when talking about his own book, said in his own inimitable way, 'I don't care what others think, I believe it's bloody brilliant!' I admired his attitude. Sometimes an incredible sense of self-belief is wonderful, as indeed it was in this case. However, failing to accept any form of external feedback can also be dangerous and self-belief can actually turn into self-delusion. (A view that's been further re-inforced by the TV programme *The X Factor*, where some members of the public have convinced themselves they have what it takes to become a pop star, despite evidence to the contrary.)

The dangers of always saying yes

How many staff have allowed themselves to be bullied because they took an overly passive approach to their boss?

How many relationships and friendships have been based more upon power and control rather than on mutual respect?

In either context, one person dominates, the other bows to the pressure. This can have far-reaching consequences. Some people, in their desire to please one person, ultimately damage their relationships with others. This can be the case particularly at work, where long hours may be continually demanded, and personal relationships at home suffer as a result. Equally, in our personal lives, the demands of friends and family may leave us feeling that we're unable to say 'no' to their requests, whilst failing to say 'yes' to our own needs. Tired and stressed out (that elastic band is beginning to weaken), you begin to feel you have no control over your life. Relationships can become strained because your constant desire to permanently please people has actually backfired.

SUMO pit stop

- How easy do you find it to say 'no'?

- Is there a relationship in or outside the workplace where you need to stop your answer always being 'yes'?

- How could you refuse someone's request without appearing impolite?

    Others respect us to the degree that we respect ourselves.

SUMO
wisdom

Another way to be OK with yourself …

4 Remember your rights and responsibilities

Recognising you and I have rights can be helpful in building better-balanced relationships with others. But what do

I mean by the term 'rights'? The best way to answer this question is to look at what these rights are, based upon the belief that people should be valued equally and treated with respect.

I have the right ...

- *To set clear boundaries*, for example, 'I need you to be aware that I am happy to work through my lunch hour but will need to leave promptly at 5p.m..'

- *To deal with others without being dependent on them for approval*, for example, 'I appreciate you don't agree with my decision, but I actually feel really good about it.'

- *To decline feeling responsible for other people's problems*, for example, 'I'd like to help you financially. However, I think you're going to have to look for ways in which you can reduce your debts.'

- *To make mistakes*, because I am not perfect.

- *To say 'no' to requests without feeling guilty or selfish*, for example, 'Thanks for the invitation, however I'm going to have to decline.'

- *To ask for time to think it over*, for example, 'There's a lot for me to consider in what you've asked. Give me 24 hours and I'll come back with a decision.'

- *To have my ideas and opinions listened to and accepted as valid for me*, for example, 'I understand this is not a priority to you, but this is an important issue for me and one I'd like us to look at.'

- *To be treated with respect* as an equal human being who may choose to be different from what others would like me to be.

- *To choose not to assert myself*, for example, to choose not to raise a particular issue.

SUMO pit stop

Review the list. If you had to identify two statements that are particularly important and relevant for you, which would they be? (I know it's tempting to ignore that last request and move on to the next part. Don't. Identifying these could have a profound affect on your relationship with others.) Is it worth writing them down and reminding yourself of them over the next couple of months?

Remember your responsibilities

Choosing to be more aware of our rights can be healthy, but our relationships with others may become unbalanced if we fail to recognise that with rights, come responsibilities. Here's another list to consider.

I have the responsibility …

- *To accept that other people have their own opinions, feelings, views and ideas, which may be different from my own* (remember the beachball).

- *To talk in a clear way to others so they understand my needs* (express your expectations).

- *To listen actively to others – even when I do not agree with them.*

- *To accept the consequences of my actions and decisions, particularly when I choose not to assert myself.*

- *To acknowledge that other people may choose not to be involved in resolving my problems.*

- *To learn from my mistakes* (listen to your Coach not your Critic).

- *To acknowledge that others may choose to be different from how I would like them to be* (Reality Rules).

- *To ensure I do not make unreasonable demands of others in order to alleviate my own stress.*

- *To regularly reflect on my own actions.*

SUMO pit stop

Again identify the two statements you most need to be aware of. What made you chose those? Do you need to have a discussion with somebody based on the statements you chose?

Your SUMO takeaway

- Building better relationships with others stems from having a healthy relationship with yourself.

- What I think about myself (insecure or steady and stable) influences how I see others – and whether I want to strangle them.

- Passive and aggressive responses to situations are both equally unhelpful. Each can arise from a sense of low self-esteem.

- Learn to be OK with you. You're a very important person.

- Four ways to be OK with yourself:

  1 Accept the positive about you.
  2 Shut Up the Inner Critic, Switch On the Inner Coach.
  3 Postpone permanently pleasing people – recognise when it is appropriate to say 'no'.
  4 Remember your rights ... and responsibilities.

- When we recognise our responsibilities in how we relate to and interact with others, it should help us be more comfortable in acknowledging our own rights. We need to be aware of both if we're to build meaningful, positive relationships with others.

Shut Up viewing yourself as second class.
Move On to giving yourself the VIP treatment.

SUMO
wisdom

**My SUMO takeaway from 'Give Yourself the VIP Treatment'
is ...**

Beware of Light Bulbs

So far we've looked at six SUMO Realities. Now for our final one. We're going to focus on the reality that no matter how hard we work at trying to improve relationships, sometimes we have to accept that certain people don't want to change. I refer to such individuals as 'light bulbs' – let me explain.

Working as a probation officer in a small town in the North of England was an enlightening experience. I saw some sights I never want to see again. I heard some stories I'd rather not recollect. At the end of my training I decided this line of work was not for me. As I applied for jobs after graduating from university, one of the most common questions I was asked was, 'Why don't you want to become a probation officer?' I mistakenly decided to give a long and convoluted answer, explaining the factors that had led to my decision. However with the interviewers interest now aroused, it wasn't uncommon to spend ten minutes of a relatively short interview, explaining (and in some cases justifying) my reasons for not pursuing such a role. Rather than taking the opportunity to sell myself and explain the reasons why I wanted to pursue a career selling women's lingerie (OK slight exaggeration – I wanted a role in Human Resources), I found myself being drawn along an avenue of questioning I didn't want to go down. Then I had a rare moment of inspiration. I simply summed up my response by tweaking a joke I'd heard.

Interviewer: So why didn't you pursue a career as a probation officer?

Me: That's a good question [as I sought to convince the interviewer they were the only person insightful enough to require such information]. Well I guess I can sum it up as follows: [sharp intake of breath as I steadied myself to deliver my killer response] 'How many probation officers does it take to change a light bulb?' [Pause whilst the interviewer tries desperately to see where this particular answer is going.] 'One – but only if the light bulb wants to change.'

OK, it wasn't meant to be funny and judging by your reaction (and most interviewers'), it wasn't. But here's the deal. It worked. Whether amused, confused or bemused, most interviewers were satisfied with my answer and moved on to another question. Result!

The story illustrates the concept I now regularly refer to as 'the light bulb', namely, a word to describe someone who is unwilling to change. And remember, Reality Rules, you will come across 'light bulbs' in life. You may even be one.

How to spot a light bulb

As with everyone, a light bulb's attitude influences their behaviour.

Here's the **TEAR** model again:

Thinking → **E**motions → **A**ctions → **R**esults

So here's a list of behaviours you may spot in a light bulb and the possible underlying attitude behind it:

- **Only being happy when they're miserable.** Some people only feel 'at home' when they have something to complain about. Being miserable has become a deeply ingrained habit (although I appreciate there may be times when a medical illness such as depression can trigger their misery). To be happy and positive would feel so unnatural that it could actually feel uncomfortable. Perhaps their beliefs are, 'I don't deserve to be happy', so when they are, this causes a certain internal conflict within them. So even when things are going well, the light bulb often passes it off with the comment, 'It'll never last.'

- **Stubbornness to the extreme.** Some people will never admit they're wrong. Their self-esteem and self-image are intrinsically linked to being seen to be always right. They mistakenly believe that if they admit they're wrong, they're undermining their own self-esteem. Stubbornness becomes a badge of honour that they wear with pride and the reason why they can never admit to being wrong.

Persistence, tenacity and refusal to give up are not the same as stubbornness.

 SUMO wisdom

- **Arguing for the fun of it.** Some people enjoy standing out from the crowd. What better way to do it than to take up a position or view that is different from everyone else? This is not done for genuine reasons (i.e. they really do disagree), but in order to meet their need for attention and personal importance. To agree with others is to become one of the crowd, and that is not something they find particularly appealing.

We all have a need to feel important and to establish our uniqueness — it's just that some people do so to the detriment of their relationships with others.

SUMO wisdom

- **A Concrete Mind.** Some people are unwilling to explore other options or possibilities. Their minds are like concrete – permanently set. They can suffer from 'selective listening syndrome' and choose what they want to hear and disregard whatever doesn't fit with their view of the world. Their resistance to opening their minds up to other people's opinions or ideas is often masked beneath a veil of cynicism.

The mind is like a parachute. It works best when it's open.

 SUMO wisdom

What often drives this behaviour is fear. People have built their view of the world on a particular foundation, and to explore alternatives could cause this foundation to crumble. Fear of such a possibility often drives people to behave in a way that actually resists examining other perspectives. Their world view is their security and they will do all they can to protect it.

The work stuff

I was running a customer care workshop for a client when two proud light bulbs arrived. Proud light bulbs (as opposed to undercover ones) often make their views, opinions and unwillingness to change very public. One individual, who worked in a customer-facing role, remarked, 'I've no idea why I'm on this course; I retire in seven years.'

His colleague sat down (having ignored my handshake of welcome when he arrived), folded his arms and asked one question at the start of the session, 'What time does this finish?'

That was his only contribution for the day.

A genuine light bulb or just a fake?

Some people are genuine light bulbs. In other words, no matter what we say or do, or what strategy we adopt, they refuse to change. But some people are fakes – they're not genuine light bulbs, they're just giving the impression they are. The issue is this: we've yet to find their right switch. Do so and you'll find that, despite initial impressions, they're actually able and willing to change.

> **SUMO wisdom**
>
> Don't write off everyone as a light bulb. There are plenty of fakes out there.

Why fake it?

A fake light bulb might be open to change, but doesn't do so for the following reasons:

- **They don't feel the need to change.** In this case, give them a good reason and they might.

- **They have yet to consider the consequences if they don't change.** When they do, they may adopt a more 'open mind'.

- **They're suffering from a mild form of SADS (Self Awareness Deficiency Syndrome).** Point out their blind spots and raise their awareness of how they're impacting others, and you might see a turnaround in their behaviour

- **Bound by belief.** They may have a genuine belief that they cannot change. They're willing to, but simply believe they can't. Give them some support, encouragement and possibly some training, and you might help them break free from their limiting beliefs.

Most people have the capacity to change. But some people either don't want to or believe they're unable to.

SUMO wisdom

SUMO pit stop

Is there anyone you live or work with who exhibits light bulb behaviour? Are they genuine or just a good fake? Is it just a case of SADS (Self Awareness Deficiency Syndrome) or something more deep rooted? If you believe they're a fake light bulb, which factor is holding them back? What action can you take to switch them on?

Recognise that there does come a time when you have to acknowledge Reality Rules and that you may need to let go and move on from a particular relationship. This means you may give up on expecting the other person to change or trying to find ways to make them do so. Have you come to this point with anyone in your life yet?

And what about yourself? Are there times when you're exhibiting light bulb behaviour?

In what areas of your life is this is most likely to occur?

How open are you to change and to letting go?

The work stuff

One manager spoke to me about how much she felt a failure because she'd had to sack a member of staff. 'I tried everything to help them improve, but none of it worked. They just didn't seem bothered.' I reassured her that there is only so much we can do to control or influence a situation. Sometimes we just need to accept that the other person does not want to change.

Your SUMO takeaway

- Light bulbs are people who refuse to change. They're not open to new ideas or considering a view point different from their own. The symptoms of light bulb behaviour include:

  - only being happy when they're miserable;
  - stubbornness to the extreme;
  - arguing for the fun of it; and
  - a concrete mind – their views are permanently set.

- Some people are not genuine light bulbs – they're fakes. They currently exhibit light bulb behaviour, but actually could change. They are capable of being switched on given enough support, encouragement and reasons to change. However we need to accept that another person's behaviour is ultimately their responsibility – and if the light bulb doesn't want to change they won't. This will be an important reality to be aware of when we're exploring how to deal with the seven SUMO Characters.

My SUMO takeaway from 'Beware of Light Bulbs' is ...

S.U.M.O. TAKEAWAY

Welcome to Part Two

The rest of this book is now devoted to the Seven SUMO Insights and the Seven SUMO Characters. Rather than write about this in two separate sections, I've weaved the insights and characters together – so we examine an insight in detail followed by a particular character for whom this may be helpful. You'll see that the more insights and tools you acquire, the more options you have in dealing with people.

A special note about the SUMO characters

When we examine a character, I'll use labels which are memorable, but which also come loaded with some negative connotations. I'm using a degree of writer's licence here. I want this material to grab you and also be remembered – the labels achieve this purpose, but I recognise they also have limitations. I'll be deliberately exaggerating and focusing on a certain part of a person's character or behaviour. Reality is, of course, somewhat different. A whole bundle of words could be used to describe us, but I'm choosing for simplicity and clarity to focus on one.

As we examine the Seven SUMO Characters, some people you know will immediately come to mind; however, it's important to realise that most of us will, at times – to varying degrees – display some of these characteristics. So it will be helpful to ask yourself not just:

- 'Who do I know that is like that?'

but also

- 'Do I sometimes demonstrate this behaviour – and if so, to what extent?'

So the names or labels may help your learning but let's make sure they do not become a language used in the character assassination of others.

Okay, let's explore our first SUMO Insight.

Arouse Your Attitude

I've come across a number of ideas on how to build rapport and develop a positive connection with other people. The advice is varied. Mirror the other person's body language; use their name; touch their elbow; nibble their ear (OK, I made the last one up). All of these tips, whilst potentially helpful, ultimately fail to address the key issue: what's your attitude like towards the other person? If you approach a colleague or a customer with the view that you're either inferior or superior in some way, that will influence how you behave towards them. The same is true with relationships outside the workplace. It doesn't matter how many tips you acquire on how to build better relationships – the starting point and foundation to developing positive, long-term relationships is your attitude towards yourself and others.

Mature people in terms of age can still be immature in terms of attitude.

> SUMO
> wisdom

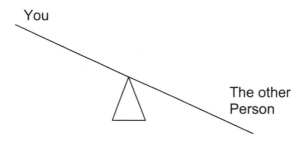

Remember the see-saw

I recently had the opportunity to work with a very well-known sports coach. I was excited at the prospect of meeting them. My friend Jeannie pointed out that however famous a person may be, we should not view them as in some way superior to us. She used the analogy of the see-saw to illustrate her point. There are three ways in which to engage in a relationship:

You

The other
Person

1. You see yourself as superior to the other person.

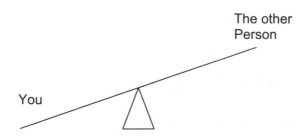

2. You see yourself as inferior to the other person..

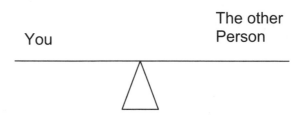

3. You see each of you to be of equal value and importance.

My initial attitude to working with this sports coach was to see him as superior to me. My thoughts before we met centred around how we could make sure our meeting was the best use of *his* time. On reflection, having decided to view our relationship as a meeting of equals, I contacted him with the question, 'How can we ensure the meeting is a good use of *our* time?'

It's easy to allow status, experience and wealth to influence how you interact with others. It's understandable. But when we start to equate people's intrinsic worth as human beings to the car they drive, their physical appearance or even ethnic background, then we have a problem. We may have opinions about people's behaviour or even their taste in clothes, but if you're interested in building successful relationships with others, take time out to reflect on your attitude. Level up that see-saw.

| SUMO wisdom | The challenge in building relationships is to see yourself as neither inferior nor superior to others. |

SUMO pit stop

Reflect on some interactions you've had with people over the last few days.

• How would you describe the see-saw in terms of how you've seen the other person in relation to yourself?

• If you felt inferior, why was that?

• If you felt superior, why was that?

• How will your approach be different when you next see that person?

The work stuff

In all humility, I think I'm a fairly nice guy. My mum brought me up well. I open doors for people. I'm courteous to other car drivers. (Unless I'm in a rush or they're displaying the club colours of Bradford City's rivals Huddersfield Town.) I genuinely seek to show respect to people I meet, which is why my next story is so out of character for me. It's an incident I will never forget. I learnt a powerful lesson.

Several years ago, I won a contract to work with an organisation that had been set up to help people who'd lost their jobs with the closure of various coal mines throughout the UK. I was hired to help people develop their CVs (or resumés), practise their interview techniques and give them the confidence to sell themselves in the job market. I enjoyed what I did and I met some great people. I also met Mark. Mark was a client with a difference. He was strange. He didn't seem to have many friends. He was a bit of a leech – he latched onto you and seemed to drain you of your life, your blood, your energy and your reasons for living. (Apart from that, he was a great bloke.) Spending five minutes with Mark felt like five hours and it became a bit of a joke amongst the consultants when he visited our office. Whilst I was on holiday, Mark's consultant left and in my absence I was assigned to look after him. He was now my client. I didn't really dislike Mark, but I slipped into the role of being the victim. None of the other consultants had wanted to work with him and it caused much amusement when I returned back from my holiday to be asked, 'Guess who's looking after Mark now that Brian's left?'

Vera the head receptionist played her part in the conspiracy. When Mark arrived to see me, she would ring through to my office and announce, 'Your friend's arrived.' Mark was in the building. What started out as a good day had just taken a turn for the worse. Then one day, I got some great news. Mark had set himself up in business. What did that mean to me? I would never see Mark again (to put this in perspective, this was the equivalent of me seeing Bradford beat Leeds and Huddersfield Town in the same week). I was thrilled. Not for him, but for me. Feeling just a little elated with the news I decided to buy the three receptionists a chocolate bar ... each. Ten minutes later my mood changed. Dramatically. As I stared out of my office window I noticed a white van arrive. I assumed it was the person to fix the photocopier. The door of the van opened. It was Mark. He was back. I dashed into the reception area. All the receptionists had eaten their chocolate. I confronted Vera.

Me: Vera, I've just seen Mark.

Vera: Yes.

Me: What's he doing back here?

Vera: Didn't you know?

Me: Know what?

Vera: Well as part of our ongoing service, Mark is now going to be using our office as his office. He'll be using our stamps, our stationary, our photocopier (when it's repaired), in fact everything. So we should be seeing a lot more of him.

As Vera spilled the bad news, a plan began to unfold in my mind – I could hide in the toilets. When Mark arrived, Vera could say I was out at lunch and he'd have to speak with another consultant. But it was too late – Mark was now standing next to me.

Mark: Hiya Paul.

Me: Hi Mark.

Mark: Can I see you for five minutes?

Me: Have you made an appointment?

Mark: No I just thought …

Me: Well you should make an appointment. I could have been see-ing another client. As it is I was just about to go for lunch.

Mark: So can I see you then?

Me: Come on then.

We walked into my office. I guess my body language was not sending out the impression that I had much enthusiasm for our unscheduled chat. We sat down opposite each other. Then Mark said something I will always remember

'I won't keep you long – because I know you don't like me.'

His words shook the walls of my complacent and uncaring attitude.

My attitude affects my behaviour and the way in which I communicate.

> SUMO
> wisdom

I was shocked at his comment. No touching of Mark's elbow, using his name or matching his body language was required. I apologised immediately.

How had I developed such an attitude towards Mark? It's not easy to explain. I guess, jokingly, all of us in the office had made Mark a figure of fun. The joke had gone too far though. He was my client. I was paid to help him. But unconsciously I'd make an arbitrary decision to provide a great service to the people I liked but less of a service to those who I didn't connect with. Maybe we all do that to an extent. It's no excuse.

On the drive back home that night I reflected on my attitude towards Mark. It had to change. It did. I made more of an effort to be friendly and welcoming. I looked less for his faults and more at his strengths. I actually found myself liking him more. He hadn't changed: I had. Our relationship improved.

I readily admit that a change in attitude will not resolve all your challenges with other people. I do believe that a few relationships have possibly reached the point of no return. But I also passionately believe that if we assess our attitude towards others, some relationships could experience significant and profound improvement.

Thanks Mark. You taught me a lot.

SUMO pit stop

Reflect on a key work relationship using the see saw as a metaphor. Which of the three see-saw illustrations best describes how you're seeing yourself and the other person within the relationship? (In terms of 'balance' I was seeing myself as superior to Mark.)

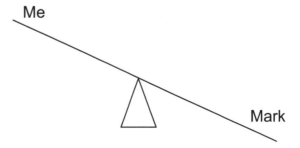

Write down you thoughts about your relationship with two people and what your current attitude towards them is like.

- What's influenced that attitude?

- How would you like your attitude to change?

Person 1

Person 2

SUMO takeaway

- Before seeking out the latest idea or technique on how to 'win friends and influence people', first check out your attitude and the judgements you make about others. When you engage with others from a position of openness and respect, you're in a far more receptive place to explore strategies on how to build a better relationship, and the ideas you do use are much more likely to be effective.

- **Shut Up** complacency.

  Move On to arousing your attitude.

My SUMO takeaway from 'Arouse Your Attitude' is …

The Ditherer

Why you may want to strangle a ditherer

As their name suggests, ditherers are not known for their deci-sive and spontaneous actions. When it comes to making deci-sions, they usually embark upon an internal wrestling match as they struggle to come up with the 'right' answer. Cautious in nature, they can exhibit hesitancy to the extreme, particu-larly when having to decide about important issues. Perhaps they mistakenly believe that if they can weigh up all the facts and leave no stone left unturned, they will discover there is a 'right' answer (and on a few occasions there may be). Put a ditherer on the spot and ask them for an instant decision and you can see the beads of sweat begin to form right before your eyes. Anxiety overtakes them and although they may come up with a quick answer, it's usually followed by a list of seven alternatives.

A ditherer in conversation in the workplace

You: So what do you think about the proposed changes to the department?

Ditherer: Er … I'm not really sure. On the one hand, it should be interesting to see if it does help customers. On the other hand, I'm still not certain if it will work. And on one hand, it's like a lot of things – it's difficult to tell.

You: That's three hands.

Ditherer: What do you mean?

You: Forget it, it doesn't matter. But haven't you studied the document put out by the board about the proposed changes?

Ditherer: Yes

You: And?

Ditherer: Well, like I said, I'm a little unsure. I need more time to weigh things up.

You: But you've had two weeks to digest the info.

Ditherer: Yeah I know, it's just so difficult to know what to think sometimes.

You: But you need to sell this idea to others in the team.

Ditherer: Oh yes I will. It's just …

You: Just what?

Ditherer: Well like I say, it's just a lot to take in and I guess I need to make up my mind what I think.

You: You certainly do. It's not going to be easy to persuade others if you're not persuaded yourself yet.

Ditherer: Yes you're right. I'll have a look at it again later. Anyway, I must go, I've got to decide which afternoon workshop I'm going to attend at the staff conference next week.

You: Which one are you thinking of?

Ditherer: I'm not sure, they all look so good. I'm hopeless at making decisions.

You: I had noticed.

A ditherer in conversation outside the workplace

You: We really need to get the bathroom sorted before we go away. Have you picked any brochures up yet?

Ditherer: Yep. I've been really busy. [Proceeds to reveal 37 brochures.]

You: That's a lot of brochures.

Ditherer: Well hopefully that will help me to decide.

You: Decide? It'll take a month to work through them!

Ditherer: No it won't. [Proceeds to lay out the brochures on the floor.]

For a start, we can eliminate these as there was nothing in them that caught my eye.

You: But that's only narrowed it down to 34 brochures.

Ditherer: Yes but I've been through them. It's just so difficult to decide. What do you think of these taps?

You: They're fine.

Ditherer: Coz I quite like these in this brochure as well. [Rummages around for the other brochure.]

You: [Now feeling overwhelmed by the amount of information and choice presented.] Er, couldn't we just go to one bathroom place and get everything from there?

Ditherer: But they might not have what we want.

You: I wasn't aware we knew what we wanted. Wouldn't it make life easier?

Ditherer: Maybe [which is a code for saying, 'No way pal']. What if we make a decision though and then once it's fitted we find something else we like?

You: Look, I'm just keen to get things moving.

Ditherer: So am I, but there's one more place I've not been to yet. Apparently they've got a great range of toilet seats.

You: [Now falling to the ground in a crumpled heap.] Look, I'm sure most seats are basically the same.

Ditherer: But let me show you this one in the 'Brighter Bathrooms' catalogue.

You: Yeah it looks great. I'm sure my bum would prefer that one to all the other ones.

Ditherer: Well we could go to one of their showrooms to have a closer look at the range and then we can compare it with others.

You: Ok. Where's the nearest one?

Ditherer: Wrexham.

You: But that's miles away, it's another flipping country!

Ditherer: But apparently Nicky's sister's husband works there and could get us a discount.

You: Ok whatever. We'll go this Saturday. Dare I ask about fire places?

Ditherer: Well, I've got some brochures …

The impact of a ditherer

Ditherers can harm their own reputation in the workplace. Their hesitancy and indecisiveness might be perceived as a major weakness and can be career-limiting. People get frustrated by ditherers. They lose confidence in people who seem riddled with uncertainty. Whether or not a ditherer has a job title of 'manager' or 'leader', developing personal leadership qualities in their personal and professional life will enhance their own satisfaction, confidence and well being. Until they do so, their behaviour will, to put it bluntly, 'frustrate the hell out of other people'.

The ditherer's side of the beachball

I hate to be wrong. I'd hate to make a decision and then find out I'd made the wrong one. That's not such a weakness is it? I hate being put on the spot – I absolutely detest it. Why rush into things and have regrets later? Have you ever done that? I know in the past I have. I guess I'm cautious in nature rather than gung-ho. I like to gather as much information and consider all the options before making a decision. I'm comfortable with this approach. The more facts you have, the easier it is to make a decision, although I have to confess, actually making a decision isn't easy.

I'm not very decisive. But I've no time for people who rush into things and don't think through the consequences. They'll live to regret it, won't they? I know I dither sometimes, but basically I'm just being thorough. Do you understand my perspective?

The work stuff

I was running a public seminar for around 40 people. They were all from different companies, but they had one thing in common. They wanted to learn more about how to successfully manage people. My one day event was a whistle stop tour of various ideas and insights that might help them to do their job more successfully. We took a lunch break. Everything seemed to be going well. I walked through reception on my way out to my car. A woman who was on the seminar caught my eye. (I later found out her name was Barbara.)

Me: Hi, enjoying the seminar?

Barbara: I'm on the wrong one.

Me: Sorry?

Barbara: I'm on the wrong one.

Me: [Thinking, well bricklaying for beginners is in the room next to ours. I guess it's an easy mistake to make.] When you say you're on the wrong one, what do you mean?

Barbara: I thought this was going to be a seminar on how to manage people.

Me: [Rather sheepishly] It is.

Barbara: Well I've come with a very specific problem and you've not covered it yet.

Me: Look, I'm really sorry. What was the problem?

Barbara: I want to know how to deal with a difficult member of staff.

Me: [Now feeling relieved] Ah, OK I see. We actually cover that topic this afternoon.

Barbara: Well I still think I'm on the wrong course. It's not what I expected.

Me: Well how can I make this afternoon a better experience for you? [Good question eh? You can tell I've done customer care training.]

Barbara: Well I'd like some advice on dealing with this member of staff.

Me: OK. I'll tell you what I'll do. Would it be alright if, when we get to the particular part of the day when we will look at dealing with difficult employees, we use your situation as a live case study? In other words, although this is a public seminar that looks at issues in a generic way, I'd be happy to tailor that part of the day to your specific situation. How does that sound?

Barbara: That would be great.

I worked really hard during the second part of the day. I wanted a satisfied customer. The section on dealing with difficult staff went well, especially the case study. At the end of the day the delegates filed out, having filled in an evaluation form which they handed to me as they left.

Barbara walked towards me. I awaited the bombardment of praise she was about to bestow on me. I tried to look humble.

Me: So how was this afternoon? [Said in a way that indicated, 'Don't hold back on the praise, I can cope, I've got broad shoulders.']

Barbara: Slightly better.

Me: Only slightly better? [I was taken aback by the distinct lack of infectious praise. Inside I was thinking, 'Doesn't this woman know how hard I've worked this afternoon to give her some ideas on how to deal with her flipping employee who she probably should never have hired in the first place?']

Barbara: I would have preferred a word-for-word script.

Me: A script?

Barbara: Yes, or a flow diagram.

Me: A flow diagram? [I was beginning to believe Barbara was in fact an actress and the whole episode was a set up.]

Barbara: Yes, a flow diagram. You ask a question of the member of staff. If they respond one way, you have a set of questions to ask, but if they respond differently, you have another set of questions. It's quite easy really.

Me: I guess I was just wanting to give you some ideas and insights on how to address the issue. I wasn't aiming to give you a prescription or a magic formula.

Barbara: Yes a script or flow diagram would have been so helpful.

Me: Well, I'm really sorry Barbara that I wasn't able to help. Have you got enough ideas though from today to at least have a meaningful conversation with this person?

Barbara: Probably not. I need to be absolutely sure that whatever I say to them will be right. I hate to be wrong. I guess I'll have to find another seminar to attend or get some more books on the subject.

Oh just in case you're wondering what the issue was that was causing Barbara all these concerns, it was … time-keeping. How long had it been going on for? About 18 months.

I used to be indecisive, but now I'm not so sure.

SUMO
wisdom

Can it ever be helpful to be a ditherer?

Yes, on occasions and up to a point. I'm quite comfortable if, when surgeons are operating to remove a kidney, they dither a little as they ascertain which one to remove. Caution can be helpful. Ditherers can be the brakes on someone else's ideas that threaten to race out of control. Their uncertainty may provide some extra time for others to reflect and ponder over their decisions. People can be provoked to ask, 'Have we explored all the options?', 'Are we jumping to conclusions or being a little hasty in our response?', etc. Applying the brakes can be useful sometimes, but you have to know when to use them. Ditherers tend to live life with their foot permanently hovering over the brake and therefore progress can be painfully slow.

How to handle not strangle a ditherer

- Recognise that their thorough and cautious nature can be of value. Do not dismiss them out of hand completely as a bunch of wimps who can never make a decision. Remember our first SUMO Insight – 'Arouse Your Attitude'.

- Where possible, limit the options ditherers have in terms of making a decision, rather than leaving their search and choice completely open-ended. For example, 'Out of these three options, which do you think will be most effective?'

- Let them know you want conclusions and clear choices rather than detailed analysis. This helps a ditherer focus on the 'ends' rather than be distracted and bogged down in the 'means'. So, for instance, state, 'By the end of your fact-finding, I want you to present what you consider to be the best three options and which one you'd personally recommend and why.'

- Back their decisions. If you believe they have made a good decision, let them know. Confidence and self belief help them to move forward with more conviction.

- Avoid, when possible, putting them on the spot and forcing them to make instant decisions. It's far more effective to give them some form of advance warning. For example, avoid, 'Right, we're running out of time now, we must make a decision, what do you think, ditherer?' Instead, 'OK, we've set aside half an hour for this meeting and by the end, we need to have made a clear decision, one way or the other.'

- Play to their strengths. Assign them tasks that do require research, but then delegate the decision-making to someone else.

- Ask questions to help them clarify their own thinking.

When a ditherer says	You might want to say
But I can't decide.	OK, let's look at your options one by one to see if we can get clarity. **OR** What do you think is holding you back from making a decision at the moment?
I'm really concerned I might be making a mistake.	Well let's look at the consequences if you do take that action. **OR** Why do you think it may be a mistake?
I'm thinking of doing X but I'm not sure.	That seems like a great option – what help do you need from me?
Maybe I should just leave things for the moment.	What's stopping you taking action now? **OR** That might well be the best thing to do – but will there be any consequences if you don't do anything now?

Questions can help clear the fog of uncertainty that clouds people's judgement.

SUMO wisdom

Handling the ditherer in yourself

1   **Shut Up** believing there is always a perfect solution.

    Move On to taking action.

2   **Shut Up** the internal conversation that says, 'I can't decide.'

    Move On to the conversation, 'I'm going to make a decision.'

3 **Shut Up** the attitude, 'I will do that tomorrow.'

Move On to, 'What's stopping me doing that today?'

4 **Shut Up** your Inner Critic who undermines your confidence.

Move On to listen to your Inner Coach who seeks to encourage you.

5 **Shut Up** doubting yourself.

Move On to believing in yourself.

SUMO pit stop

- What decisions do you tend to dither over?

- What do you think are the reasons why you can be indecisive?

- When has being cautious been helpful?

- What would help you be more decisive? (Have you read the 'Learn Latin' principle in my first SUMO book? If not, you may find it helpful and if you have, it may be worth re-reading.)

- If you live or work with a ditherer, which strategy or insight will help you move on in your relationship with them?

Humility Helps

We live in a competitive world. We always have. In the early days of mankind's existence we competed for food. Our goal was survival. In some parts of the world it still is. But for many of us, our needs now seem much more complex. We're competing to climb the career ladder, or to win business in the new global economy. Many of us also compete for prestige and power. We want to be significant. We need to feel important and to feel that our lives count. And the way to achieve all this? Well the message seems fairly clear. Put yourself first, make sure your needs are met. Look after number one. After all, if you want to be the best, that's what it's going to take.

And now I guess you're expecting self righteous Paul McGee to condemn such selfish attitudes. Right? Wrong. I actually believe that we do have to consider our own needs. As I quoted earlier, 'Love your neighbour as yourself.' It's difficult to love (in the widest meaning of the word) your neighbour (who in my definition is not just the person you live near to, but potentially everyone you encounter) if you don't love yourself.

I do a lot of flying and the airlines have clued into this concept. If there's a loss of air pressure inside the plane, then oxygen masks appear. However, the safety announcement clearly states, 'Fit your own oxygen mask first before helping others.' (The point being presumably that you're in a better position to help others once you have enough oxygen yourself.)

So if I'm actually agreeing that we need to consider our own needs, where exactly does humility come into all this? If, as I've argued, we do live in a competitive world, then what part can humility play in helping our relationship with others? After all, it's such a weak concept isn't it? Yes it is – if your definition of humility is, 'Don't stand up for your rights, other people's needs are more important than yours, be submissive, don't answer back, play small.' But what if the definition of humility relates more to the following?

- 'Look out for the needs of others as well as your own.

- Recognise you need help from others.

- Acknowledge your mistakes.

- Say sorry when you get things wrong.

- Apologise and ask for forgiveness when necessary.

- Understand you don't know everything and have much to learn.

- Accept others may have a valid point of view even when it differs from yours.'

That definition puts a different light on things doesn't it?

SUMO wisdom

Humility is not about thinking any less of yourself, it's about thinking of yourself less.

To be humble is not about putting yourself down in order to elevate others. As we explored in 'Arouse Your Attitude', it's simply an awareness that, whatever a person's age, gender, skin colour, race or religion, we are all of equal importance and value. Our contribution to society, our abilities, our levels of intelligence and the amount of wealth we have may all vary, but at the very core of our being, we all have the same worth. I may feel more important because of the car I drive or the house I live in, but ultimately, my physical needs are the same as everyone elses. I still need to eat (in my case, regularly), to wash (in my case, occasionally) and go to the toilet (in my case, excessively). However I digress. Let's examine how an attitude and approach to life that involves more humility and less arrogance can help us build better relationships with others.

Humility in practice

The first way to develop humility ...

Think about the needs of others

Want to improve your service to customers? Think about their needs rather than putting your company's needs first. There are thousands of books written about customer service, but ultimately, if we can develop the cultural mindset, 'How can we best meet and exceed the needs of our customers and provide them with a product or service that they'll gladly pay for?', then we're laying the foundations for a successful, long-term business.

The work stuff

A leading British retailer developed what many considered at the time to be an arrogant attitude towards its customers. They refused to accept payment for goods by credit card, unless it was the store's own credit card. They certainly lost my business when, having approached the till armed with a dozen new pairs of undergarments (well it had been twenty six years since the last new set, so I sensed it was time for a change), I realised they wouldn't accept my credit card and I had insufficient cash to pay. Alas I had to return the extra large elasticated 'Y' fronts back to whence they came. It seemed that the company's policy in terms of methods of payment was designed to meet their needs and not that of the customer. Thankfully, they recognised the error of such an attitude and changed their stance on credit cards. Many business analysts believe this particular retailer has seen an increase in profit because they ditched their arrogant approach and now spend more time listening to their customers. I guess you could say their humility lead to increased profitability.

In my own work as a presentation coach, I constantly have to remind presenters of the best way to overcome nerves. Nerves are not necessarily a bad thing (it's OK to experience butterflies in your stomach, you just need to teach them how to fly in formation), but they often stem from being too focused on ourselves. In our mind, the focus can be, 'What will the audience think of me? What if I make a mistake? What if I forget something?' I get the presenter to think more about the needs of the audience and to recognise the aim of their presentation is about serving and helping the audience in some way. When they become more externally focused and think less about their own needs, most people begin to relax more.

It's also important to think of the needs of others in a personal context. The writer and speaker Jeff Lucas inspired the following, challenging piece of wisdom:

SUMO wisdom

Shut Up self absorption.
Move On to noticing and caring for the needs of others.

The second way to develop humility ...

Ask for help
Whatever people achieve in life, no-one can put their success **entirely** down to their own efforts. In business and in life, we need the support of others. Sometimes that is seen in obvious ways such as through the help of a manager, coach or mentor, but sometimes, it can be less direct. Support comes through the person who booked the meeting room, prepared your slides, ordered you some lunch, checked you in for your flight or repaired your car.

SUMO wisdom

No one gets to the top solely on their own efforts — although some people would like to think that was the case.

Humility is about recognising you don't have all the answers and we do have limitations. Those who fail to recognise this will appear arrogant and can be susceptible to burn-out; not exactly a great combination for achieving successful relationships. Great questions to ask others might include:

- • 'Look, I could really do with some help or advice – do you have a few minutes to spare?'

- • 'If you were me in this situation, what would you do?'

The work stuff

I'm a great follower of sport. When it comes to supporting my national team, England, I can become the world's greatest enthusiast about anything if there's a chance of England winning it. Sometimes, this has meant adopting an interest in a range of sports that I would not normally entertain, but if England are one of the world's best at playing dominoes, then I will cheer them on. However, back in November 2003, I was able to celebrate a more meaningful England triumph when they won the Rugby Union World Cup in Australia. What made the victory even more sweet is that the triumph was actually achieved in Australia. The England team was coached by Clive Woodward, who, shortly after our memorable victory, was knighted and became Sir Clive Woodward. I picked up his book called *Winning* a few months back and was impressed by how he'd implemented a number of ideas that helped England to ultimately achieve world cup success. I decided to write to Sir Clive, thanking him for such a great book and also enclosing a copy of my SUMO book. Within 24 hours he'd emailed me to thank me and shared how he'd already used the phrase 'Shut Up, Move On' at work. A few weeks later he contacted me to ask if we could meet up as he wanted to pick my brains and explore some more of my SUMO ideas. Despite achieving incredible success both within business and sport, Sir Clive Woodward was still eager and humble enough to realise you never stop learning and was willing to seek help from someone who, by comparison, was relatively unknown.

SUMO pit stop

1   Think about some of your key relationships. Have you been considering other people's needs recently? Is there someone you could contact today with no other agenda than to simply ask how they are? (Could this be a good approach with your boss, a member of the team or perhaps a customer?)

2   Faced with a challenge, how willing are you to ask for help? Is there someone you could approach today for their support and advice?

The third way to develop humility ...

Apologise and acknowledge mistakes

Speak to anyone who knows me and there will be a common agreement about the assessment of my character. When it comes to relationships, Paul McGee still has much to learn. That's not me trying to appear all humble, it's just a fact. My humour can sometimes cause offence, I still find myself judging people too quickly and I can allow fatigue and my natural tendency towards impatience to influence my decision-making without really thinking through the consequences.

> **SUMO wisdom**
> It's always useful to remember that we're all a work in progress ... it's just that some people are progressing faster than others.

But here's one thing I have learnt and am making some progress on – I find a willingness to admit my mistakes and apologise when necessary is incredibly helpful in 'moving on' a relationship. Some relationships remain gridlocked simply because no one is prepared to admit they've made a mistake or done something wrong. Sadly, in our litigious society, an unwillingness to admit our guilt or to make an apology is driven by the threat of possible legal action. It's a sad fact of life, but one we do need to be aware of. However, although such a response may be advisable in certain circumstances, surely it doesn't have to affect **every** area of our lives? I actually know that saying sorry with real meaning and sincerity can be incredibly powerful in helping to heal a relationship.

Acknowledging your mistake and apologising (when there is cause to do so) applies the brakes to escalating relationship problems.

SUMO wisdom

SUMO pit stop

- How good are you at acknowledging that you've made a mistake?

- Is there anyone in your life at present you need to apologise or say sorry to?

The work stuff

As a business, we've spent several thousand pounds on printing over the years. One company who initially did our printing are no longer in business. Although I have no idea why this is the case, I am clear on why we became a *former* customer. They did some printing for us and made a mistake. They didn't deny they had made a mistake. Neither did they apologise. In fact we were made to feel guilty for complaining. Our whole experience left us feeling let down and uncomfortable in dealing with them. Contrast that with an organisation called the Philo Trust. I love to listen to a fellow motivational speaker J. John. Having ordered one of his CDs, I was enjoying listening to his words of wisdom until the CD ceased to work. I was frustrated and disappointed. When I contacted the organisation, they were quick to apologise. (They also avoided using the phrase which really annoys me, 'Well no one else has complained of that problem.' Quite frankly I don't care how many people complain about a problem. I have an issue and I want it sorting.) Within 24 hours my replacement CD arrived along with a handwritten apology and an additional complimentary product. The Philo Trust are still in business. It's hardly rocket science, is it?

SUMO wisdom

Remember the Four 'A's:
Acknowledge your mistake.
Apologise.
Offer an Alternative solution.
Then Action it.

The personal stuff

Occasionally when I annoy Helen, she wants to give me some 'constructive feedback'. On this occasion she prepared a 416-page report against me, the accused, and she was looking forward to presenting her findings. And then what do I go and do? I admit liability and confess my guilt. There is no case for the defence. My conviction is sealed within seconds. Helen is disarmed and frustrated ... she'd only just got going. But here's the reality:

SUMO wisdom

Saying sorry can release relationship deadlock.

Despite Helen's initial frustration at my early capitulation (which I only do if I genuinely feel I am in the wrong), her anger does begin to subside and we're in a better position to 'move on'. However, here's an important lesson. **True humility is not simply admitting your mistake and apologising, it's also about taking action to ensure the same mistake is not repeated.**

Powerful phrases may include, 'You're right, that was completely out of order' or 'I'm genuinely sorry for the hurt/delay/anguish that's been caused. Here's what I'm going to do ...'

The fourth way to develop humility ...

Welcome feedback
In my line of work as a speaker, delegates are often asked to give their feedback. It's always useful to receive as it gives

me the opportunity to reflect on what people took from my message and also get their views on how things could be improved. But my experience is not the norm and most of us rarely receive feedback from others unless it's in the form of an appraisal at work. Outside of work, it would be quite unusual – some would even say bizarre – to sit down and discuss with your partner, children or friends what their thoughts are concerning you behaviour. These people usually have more subtle and indirect ways of letting you know what they think of you.

However, whatever your position at work and role in life, be prepared to seek out and listen to feedback from others. At work, don't simply expect to receive feedback from your boss, but also from your peers and colleagues. You might not agree with all that you hear and you do need to weigh up and reflect on the comments you receive; but this exercise can provide you with a fascinating opportunity to gain an insight into what others think of you. Remember also that feedback is not just about focusing on your 'areas for development' (a term previously know as weaknesses): it's also designed to highlight your strengths.

Here are a few questions you might ask others in order to gain some feedback. They're not intended to be prescriptive, but to stimulate some food for thought. What you ask depends on how comfortable you already are in the relationship.

With a customer

- 'Is there anything myself or the team could do to help improve our service to you?'

- 'What is it about our service that you particularly appreciate? What can we do to sustain that?'

- 'If you had to describe our service to someone, what would you say?'

With your boss

- 'Is there an area of my work I need to be giving more attention to at the moment?'

- 'Is there anything you particularly want me to focus on at this time?'

- 'Boss, if you had to give a totally honest reference about me what would you say?'

With your staff

- 'If there was one thing you could change about me, what would it be?'

- 'What's the most positive attribute I have as a manager?'

- 'How can I help you do an even better job?'

With your partner

- 'What is it about our relationship that you particularly value?'

- 'If there was one thing I need to be aware of that would enhance our relationship, what would it be?'

- 'If you had to describe me in four words, what would they be?'

Sometimes getting feedback is not a comfortable experience.

The following was inspired by Michael Neil, author of the best-selling book *You Can Have What You Want* and is used with his permission.

> *According to author Steven K. Scott, every piece of criticism we receive contains water, sand and gold. The water is the noise in the criticism – the part of the criticism which washes over*

*you with little effect. The sand is the bit that stings – the part
of the criticism you find virtually impossible not to take personally – the stuff that hurts. The gold is the nugget of truth in
the criticism – the piece that if you took it to heart, you would
be able to change things for the better. While panning for the
gold in a particularly harsh criticism can be difficult, the effort
is inevitably worthwhile.*

Interesting stuff I thought, so I applied it to some feedback
I received recently about my SUMO philosophy. The email
read:

*Yet another self-help guru who reckons he's got all the an-
swers. Just like the American charlatans, you promise people
the earth but then leave them disappointed. Your ideas lack
any originality or substance – it's all been said before. When
will you stop exploiting the needy and the stupid and start
being honest for once?*

I was shocked and deeply saddened when I read it. However
using the water, sand and gold technique I was able to view
this 'feedback' in a more constructive way.

Water: Phrases like 'self–help guru' and 'American Charlatans'
were easy to allow to wash over me.

Sand: I guess the phrase that hurt was, 'Your ideas lack any
originality or substance'. I recognise that there is nothing new
under the sun, but I work hard at putting my message together in an original way. I appreciate my SUMO philosophies
are simple, but I have received so much positive feedback regarding how helpful they have been that I strongly reject the
argument that they lack substance.

Gold: The phrase, 'When will you stop exploiting the needy'.
This made me realise that when I speak, there will be needy
people in my audience. They may be hurting and desperately
seeking answers. I need to remind myself that my career as a

speaker and author is a privilege, but it's also a responsibility – one that I should never take lightly.

Your SUMO takeaway

Humility can give you the competitive advantage in life. It can enhance relationships. It's not about putting yourself down and considering others better than you. It's about recognising your worth *and* that of others. Develop your humility by:

- thinking about the needs of others;

- asking for help;

- apologising and admitting mistakes; and

- welcoming feedback.

SUMO wisdom

Shut Up inappropriate pride.
Move On with humility.

My SUMO take-away from 'Humility Helps' is …

S.U.M.O. TAKEAWAY

The Commander

Why you may want to strangle a commander

Firstly a confession. I'm a little uncomfortable writing about this character. Why? I relate to a lot of their characteristics. It's quite strange to be writing about a difficult person when you realise that in many ways you're writing about yourself. But here goes anyway. (If you've read SUMO, you'll already know a little about this character.)

Commanders like to get things done. No harm in that, is there? Unfortunately this desire to see things achieved – sometimes at all costs – can make them difficult to deal with. The words 'patience' and 'relaxation' are as common to their world as are three straight wins for Bradford City. Commanders love 'to-do lists'. They get a buzz out of completing tasks. They've even been known to complete tasks that were not on their original 'to-do list' – and then write them on (even though they're already completed) so they can then have the thrill of crossing them off. For a commander, the feeling of getting things done is akin to being able to break wind after an evening in the company of others – so very necessary and so very satisfying. (Or is that just me?)

Their single-minded focus can at times make them vulnerable in the area marked 'beware of other people's feelings'. People, quite frankly, can get in the way. And the tough demands they make of themselves are often expected of others. Energy and drive are to be found in abundance – tolerance and sensitivity less so. Commanders enjoy quick wins and progress. Long-term tasks where results may take time to see are less enthusiastically embraced. Lack of interest, boredom and disengagement can occur when progress is slower than expected.

A commander in conversation in the workplace

Commander: Ok I've got a few minutes between meetings, so fire away.

You: Well I'm feeling a little stressed at the moment.

Commander: Sorry to hear that.

You: And I just need someone to talk about it.

Commander: OK, I'm all ears.

You: Well I wanted to discuss my current levels of workload.

Commander: Are you saying you can't cope with the amount?

You: Well, not exactly.

Commander: Then what are you saying?

You: Well I think, it's just that …

[Phone rings.]

Commander: Sorry, it's an urgent call, won't be a moment.

[Delay of two minutes whilst the commander resolves the oil crisis in the Middle East.]

Commander: Apologies for that. Anyway you were saying?

You: Well I was wondering if it might be possible to get a little more admin support?

Commander: I'm sure we can sort something out on that front. Have a word with Jenny.

You: Thanks.

Commander: Good, that's that sorted. Was there anything else?

You: Em … [You take two seconds to reflect, but before you can add anything …]

Commander: Great. Well, look I must dash. I'm meeting Terry shortly and then I've got a conference call with the States at 5 p.m. Anyway, let me know how you get on.

You: Er ... yes, I will.

The commander then turns to their daily to-do list and ticks off the task 'Have a meeting with distressed employee'. There is an inner glow as they do so – a feeling which is further enhanced by the fact that the meeting finished slightly ahead of schedule.

A commander in conversation outside the workplace

You: Are you alright?

Commander: Yes, it's just that my waters have broken. You better call an ambulance, looks like the baby is coming.

You: OK. I'll do that straight away. Can I get you anything in the meantime?

Commander: Yes, pass me my laptop, there's a couple of emails I just want to finish. And have you seen my phone? I promised Jacksons I'd get back to them by 4 p.m.

You: But you're in labour. You're about to give birth. Can't these things wait?

Commander: Look, it will be at least ten minutes before the ambulance arrives ... might as well use my time productively. I've got everything ready for the hospital. I've made a list of all that I need and who I need to contact. Anyway, enough of my ramblings, we're using up valuable time here. Honestly I hope this baby doesn't decide to take its time.

The impact of a commander

Although a commander's style may motivate and inspire some people, our focus here is on the potential negative impact of their behaviour. In some cases, people can feel ignored and undervalued by a commander. They may feel their views and opinions are not being listened to. Emotions can be swept aside, as the commander takes the steam roller approach to moving things forward. The task will be completed – but at what price? Morale can be undermined and people can feel overworked as they seek to keep up with the relentless pace of a commander. No sooner has one job been done, than the commander is thinking about the next one. Reflection and rest can be rare.

The assertive style of commanders can be seen by some as verging on bullying. Problems may be dealt with, but people will not always feel valued or cared for. A person's indecisiveness will be seen as a weakness by the commander and people may lack the confidence to articulate their feelings to them. Even when they do, a commander usually has a quick response.

The commander's side of the beachball

So what's wrong with being fast and focused? Life is too short, and time too valuable, to be wasted. My mantras are 'seize the day' and 'make it happen'. They've served me well. Look what I've achieved.

Frankly, some people spend too long planning and not enough time doing. In my opinion, some organisations are drowning in meetings. Can you relate to that where you work?

I'm not here simply to talk about stuff, I want to get things done. If people think my pace is a little too fast for them, the onus is on them to speed up. Why should I have to slow down? When there's a crisis, what are we supposed to do? Have a planning meeting and take a vote?

Can you see where I'm coming from?

And when I'm accused of not being a good listener, I just wish people would get to the point – I don't 'do' waffle. As for small talk – that's for parties. I really am truly sorry if your pet cat was unwell over the weekend, but I've got clients to satisfy and business to win. Am I impatient? Possibly. But as I see it, that's more to do with the dithering, laid back nature of others. I'm here to make things happen and take decisions – even the hard ones.

If people don't like my style, then I'm afraid that's their problem. It's utter rubbish when you accuse me of not caring. It's because I care that I'm driven to take action. I want to do something to turn things around and improve a situation. Does that make sense?

The work stuff

I was running a workshop for managers called 'How to get the best from your team'. Ian, one of my delegates, didn't seem to care much for people. His god was results. He worshipped them. As a sales manager, it could be argued that's what he was paid for. He confessed, in his words, that his 'firm but fair' approach had won few friends and a high staff turnover. He was looking for answers – fast.

Even during the introductions at the start of the workshop Ian seemed impatient. Rather than seeing this as a chance to build rapport and relax the group, he saw it more as a necessary evil to be endured at the start of a training session. To be fair, he listened intently. It was only a one-day course. (Well, commanders would rarely have time for a longer one.) We examined a number of ideas to help motivate others.

In the afternoon of the workshop, we discussed more about the people delegates considered a challenge on their team. Ian talked about

Dan. Dan was new to the business, had bags of enthusiasm, but had yet to perform to the level Ian required. The conversation about how Ian would deal with Dan went something like this:

Me: So Ian, what's your approach going to be with Dan?

Ian: Well, like you said Paul, I need to find an appropriate time and place for our discussion.

Me: Good. That's hugely important. How will you start the meeting?

Ian: 'Dan, you have the potential not to be crap.'

Me: Sorry, what did you say?

Ian: 'You have the potential not to be crap.'

Me: Right, that's what I thought you'd said. Ian do you want to think about your use of language when speaking to Dan?

Ian: You mean the word 'potential'?

Me: I was thinking more of the word 'crap'. For someone who's a sales manager I thought you might be good at finding the right words to say.

Ian: Look. I don't believe in beating around the bush. He needs to know the score. It's a complete waste of time waffling around the issue.

I was never sure whether Ian was being genuinely serious or simply trying to wind me up, but I suspect the former. The example illustrates extreme commander behaviour. What concerns me is some readers just read the above and thought, '"The potential not to be crap" ... em, I like that phrase. Could come in handy during my next staff performance review meeting.'

Can it ever be helpful to be a commander?

Speaking as someone who has a tendency to exhibit some of these traits on occasions, I would have to shout a loud YES. In fact organisations need commanders to drive things forward.

When meetings are getting bogged down or when people are going round in circles, then the need for someone to take control is both obvious and necessary. During a crisis, there's not always enough time to consider people's feelings or opinions and a more autocratic approach may be needed to salvage the situation. At home, when the house resembles a builder's scrap yard, I feel that the need to 'do commander' seems more appropriate than 'do committee'.

The personal stuff

We were due to visit some friends one Saturday afternoon. They asked us to arrive for about 3p.m. In my world, 'about 3 p.m.' does not equate to 3.30 p.m., but allows us a little slack as to the precise time we arrive. It takes about ten minutes in the car to get to our friends' house. At 3.15 we're still standing in the hallway, attempting what is proving to be an almost insurmountable problem – getting two adults and two children (aged three and five at the time) into the car. Half an hour previously, I was 'Mr Relaxed'; now I was definitely 'Mr Commander'. The conversation went something like this:

Me: Come on, we're already late. I won't tell you again, put your shoes on. [This was not addressed to Helen, but my two young children.]

Ruth: Daddy, I want to wear my Snow White dress.

Me: Ruth, we haven't got time darling, we need to go.

Ruth: [Strangely not responding to my adult logic.] But I want my Snow White dress.

Me: Ruth put your shoes on and get into the car. [I can make Rambo look laid back at times.]

Ruth now falls to the floor sobbing. The commander decides to ignore this act of defiance and turns to his next target.

Me: Matthew, how many times have I told you? Put your Game Boy away and get your coat.

Five minutes later, calm has almost been restored. Ruth is sulking, her sobbing though has diminished and father and daughter have reached an uneasy truce. It's now 3.20. We're about to leave. Then ...

Helen: Oh, Dave and Jenny left a message. They just want us to confirm that we are OK for Sunday tea tomorrow.

Me: Helen, we agreed this last week. They know we're coming.

Helen: Yes I know, but Jenny just wanted us to confirm. I'll give her a quick call while I remember.

Me: Helen [said in a 'don't make me angry, you wouldn't like me when I'm angry' tone of voice], we're twenty minutes late and we haven't left yet. Ring Dave and Jen when we get back.

Helen: [Oblivious to the volcano ready to erupt before her.] Well we said 'about 3 p.m.'. I'll ring them now whilst I remember.

I stare at my watch in an act of desperation. It doesn't work. Helen goes to pick up the phone. If I'd made the call (which on reflection I should have done), the conversation would have been over in seven seconds or less. But not with Helen, she even walks more slowly to the phone. She might as well be wearing a T-shirt saying, 'Chill out commander, what's the rush?' I could only hear Helen's side of the phone conversation. It went like this:

'Hi Jen. How are you? Good. How's Dave? Really? Oh. What happened then? Amazing. How's Katie?' (At this point I find solace in the fact that Katie is their only child. If they had a larger family, I would have lost the plot completely.) However, it's Helen's next question that tips me over the edge. 'So what have you been doing today then?' Let's just say my response in the background betrayed the fact that I was the author of the book *59 Minutes To A Calmer Life*. I came close to head-butting the wall. I proceeded to grab the children (gently of course) and storm off out to the car. My exasperation with Helen was taken out on the car seat as I fought to secure Ruth into the back seat. Helen and I sat in silence during the journey. We arrived at 3.35. Our friends greeted us at the door with smiles that actually gave the impression they were happy to see us. They never mentioned the time. I switched back into 'Mr Almost Normal' mode and we had a good afternoon. Next day we had a cracking meal at Dave and Jen's. We were late again of course, but no one made too much of a deal – except me of course.

How to handle not strangle a commander

- Remember a commander's behaviour is driven by a desire to get things done and not to put people down. But if left unchecked, commanders have the potential to bully you. Stand up to them and make them aware of how they're coming across.

- Avoid being subtle. Be direct. Commanders can cope and eventually appreciate you being direct and to the point with them.

- Be sensitive when you want to talk with a commander and you sense they're busy. Start by asking, 'Is this a good time?' If it's not, be clear you need to speak to them and agree when would be a good time.

- Think before you speak. If you only had a minute of a commander's time, what would be the main thing you'd want to communicate? It's also helpful to communicate in a logical, structured way. For instance, 'OK I've got three points I want to make. The first is …; Secondly I think it's important that …; And finally …'

We all appreciate clarity, commanders in particular.

- Remind them it's about 'the people' as well as 'the task' and to make sure they have some fun along the way. Helen will often say to me:

  - 'Take a chill pill, commander.'
  OR
  - 'I think you could have shown a little more compassion with the kids over that issue.'

- Remember not all commanders are managers. If they're part of your team, make sure you give them responsibility for certain tasks, otherwise they can become easily bored.

If a commander says	You might want to say …
Can I just stop you at that point?	Actually I haven't quite finished yet
Come on, we're wasting time here.	Can I make you aware of how you're coming across to me at the moment.
But we have to meet the deadlines.	You're right, we do and we need to quickly consult staff on how best we can manage this.
No-one minds if we do it this way, do they?	Thanks for asking – actually I do mind. Can I make another suggestion?

Handling the commander in yourself

1 **Shut up** focusing solely on the task.

   Move On to considering the needs of others.

2 **Shut Up** believing action is always necessary.

   Move On to recognising the benefit of rest and reflection.

3   **Shut Up** being so single-minded.

Move On to seeing the other side of the beachball.

4   **Shut Up** sometimes.

Move On to Listening Loud more often.

SUMO pit stop

- Do you spend regular time with a commander?

- How does their behaviour impact your relationship?

- What's your approach in dealing with them? (For further advice on the above, please contact my wife, Helen.)

- If you recognise many of the commander traits in yourself, what can you do to lessen the negative impact of your behaviour?

Listen Loud

Sir John Harvey-Jones is a former Chairman of ICI. When it comes to leadership, he's regarded as something of a guru. He's credited with having said the following:

If I could wave a magic wand and give managers any ability, I would give them the ability to listen. Most managers are good at talking, but good communication requires both.

Listening is a fundamental skill when you want to build better relationships with others. In reality, most of us are pretty lousy at it. And I think we're getting worse. The increasing pace of life means we now seem to have even less time to give other people our attention. Not only that, but most people's behaviour, including my own, sometimes gives the impression that our definition of 'listening' is 'waiting for my turn to talk'.

The challenges of being a good listener

Biology

When it comes to listening, we're biologically challenged. Experts seem to disagree on the exact figures, but they do agree with the following:

You can process and think through information a lot faster than someone else can speak.

The figures I've come across are that most people speak, on average, 150 words per minute, but we can think and process up to 600 words per minute. In simple terms, when you're speaking to someone, they have the ability to think four times faster than you can speak. Let me give you an example of how this fact manifests itself in day to day life.

Have you ever been introduced to someone and moments later thought: 'What was their name again?' If your answer is a resounding 'yes', then join the club.

So why does this happen?

When you meet someone for the first time, your brain is instinctively trying to suss out the other person. At a very basic level, we're asking the question, 'Friend or foe?' Our brain is also processing thousands of other pieces of information around the core question – what's this person like? What can I tell about them based on age, height, eye contact, strength of hand shake, smell?

This is all happening unconsciously.

Coupled with all this, we're also entering into a formal ritual whereby we meet, greet and give our names. The brain is now working overtime trying to analyse all this information, as well as deciding what to say next after we've heard the other person's name.

It's not so much that we forget the other person's name, but more the case that we're not concentrating or paying attention when they say it.

The personal stuff

A few years ago, I'd just finished delivering a seminar in Nottingham. It had been a challenging day. The group seemed to contain an above average number of 'light bulbs'. Feeling a little bit sorry for myself, I got into my car to drive to my next venue. I switched on the radio. The very first words I heard were:

'The British BBC Television presenter ...' I knew immediately by the tone of voice that some very sad news was about to come. Before the announcer could finish his sentence, my mind had clicked into overdrive.

- Who was this person?
- What had happened?

A picture immediately came to mind. I was aware that Helen Rolla-son, a sports reporter and presenter for the BBC, was ill with cancer. Her prognosis was not good. Whilst my brain was anticipating her name, the announcer completed his sentence ...

'... Jill Dando was today shot and killed outside her home.'

It was a tragic and unexpected event. It also illustrated how quickly our mind works when someone is talking. It's not easy to be a good listener.

Attitude

It's all too easy to allow your attitude towards another person to become a barrier to what they're saying. With some people, we decide to switch off as soon as they start talking. It's not so much a question of finding it difficult to listen, but deciding not to listen.

A friend of mine said recently, 'I never listen to a word politi-cians say – they're all full of crap.'

Although some people may have some sympathy with such a view, it's also one that can pervade a range of relationships, from family gatherings to team events. Perhaps we need to be honest and humble enough to recognise that although we might not normally agree with the other person, it's worth staying open-minded, at least initially, to what they have to say.

The work stuff

An organisation was having to make a number of staff redundant. As part of their leaving package, I had been invited to share some of my

SUMO principles in order to help staff come to terms with what had happened and also to prepare them for the future. One of the organisers mentioned in the invitation that my style was 'motivational'. One member of staff refused to attend the session. In an email, he wrote

'The very thought of listening to a motivational speaker turns my blood cold.'

The event was a great success and all staff left clutching a copy of my SUMO book. One person's attitude had of course meant that he didn't get to listen to my ideas. That's his choice, but in all honesty (and a small dash of humility), I think he missed out.

A third factor that makes listening a challenge is:

Distraction

My office is at home. That has its advantages, but also its drawbacks.

Matt and Ruth will occasionally come into my office when I'm working and tell me their news. Matt usually to tell me which player he's just signed on his football manager game and Ruth to tell me some story, usually recounted in great detail, from her day.

I've realised that when they do this, I cannot listen in any meaningful or engaging way if I'm typing emails when they're talking. I have to make a decision. Either I listen half-heartedly whilst continuing to work, or I stop what I'm doing, swivel my chair round and focus on them.

Distractions destroy our ability to listen effectively to others. Whilst some distractions may be unavoidable, others occur because we lack the desire or discipline to stop them.

The personal stuff

England were playing a World Cup game. I was working away from home and staying in a hotel. England were losing. The game was poor. I rang Helen from my bedroom with the match still on in the background. She'd had a difficult day. She was after some sympathy and understanding. England equalised. My response to her difficult day?

'Yes! Get in there, son. Well done.'

I now switch the television off when ringing home. The consequences of not doing so are unprintable.

What people often crave, is not somebody to talk to them, but someone who is willing to listen.

SUMO wisdom

How to Listen Loud

We've explored some of the potential barriers to listening to others, now let's find out how to improve our ability.

It's your choice

When I'm running workshops, I don't use name cards. I make an effort to concentrate when I'm introduced to people and listen and repeat their names. I then write their name down. (Admittedly, it is easier for me to do this within this context as delegates may be expecting me to make a note of their name.) My goal is that by the time my workshop starts, I have remembered everyone's name. It's a short term strategy, but it works. It helps me engage on a more personal level with the group.

My memory is no better than anyone else's, yet people regularly ask 'How do you remember everyone's name?' I have no magic wand formula, but the key is this – it's down to my attitude. I make a decision *before* the workshop starts to try and remember everybody's name. I make the effort. My alternative? I could chose to become a victim of the C.I.B.A. (Can I Be Ars*d) Syndrome.

> **SUMO wisdom**
>
> *The ability to listen well begins with a genuine desire to do so.*

Put on a show

It's important to show that you're listening as perception is reality here. If I believe that you're listening to me, then as far as I'm concerned, you are. However, if you give me the impression you're not listening (even if you are), my perception becomes my truth. Therefore it's important not only to listen, but through your body language (and a few encouraging noises), to make the other person aware that you are.

> **SUMO wisdom**
>
> *Beware blanket statements about body language. In some cultures, avoiding eye contact is a sign of respect.*

Play detective

Please don't get the wrong impression and think that listening is 'the art of saying nothing'. There will be times when it is very appropriate to interrupt, play detective and ask relevant, probing questions in order to gain a clearer understanding of what is being said.

I often illustrate this idea by introducing the TED principle (**T**ell, **E**xplain and **D**escribe) when it comes to asking questions. Let me elaborate.

'Could you **T**ell me more about that?' People may only give you some of their story, forgetting you might not have as much information as they do. This question helps facilitate the sharing of more general information and aids your understanding of the bigger picture.

'Why don't you **E**xplain that to me?' This question provides an opportunity for people to elaborate in more detail about a specific issue.

'**D**escribe that to me.' This helps provide a clearer picture in terms of what actually happened when someone is describing an event.

The goal in asking probing questions is not to put people on the defensive, but to gain a clearer and more accurate view of a situation.

SUMO wisdom

State their case

A great way to show that you've listened and sought to understand another person's perspective is to take a little time to replay back the main points you've just heard. Do this before stating your view. It's a great way to clarify what you've just heard and also communicate understanding. For example 'What I understand you to be saying is ... Have I got that right or have I missed something?'

The personal stuff

I think an area where listening to others is often overlooked is in relation to parents with their children. It's something Helen and I are working on. We recognise that, as children, Matt and Ruth have views and opinions of their own. They may lack experience or maturity (well Helen's maturity anyway), but they should still be respected for how they see things.

Helen and I make mistakes.

I recently failed to respond to Ruth's behaviour in quite the calm but assertive way I would have liked. I overreacted. Whilst reflecting on one of my SUMO questions, 'Is my response appropriate and effective?', I realised it wasn't. The punishment hadn't fitted the crime. When we'd both calmed down, I decided to chat with Ruth on our own. The conversation went something like this:

Me: Ruth how do you feel about what happened before?

Ruth: Sad.

Me: In what way?

Ruth: Because you shouted.

Me: OK but do you know why I was cross?

Ruth: Yes.

Me: Why was I cross darling?

Ruth: Because I hadn't tidied my bedroom.

Me: That's right. But I'm sorry for getting angry. I shouldn't have shouted so much. Do you forgive me?

Ruth: Yes. [Avoiding eye contact.]

Me: Are you sure darling?

Ruth: Yes.

Me: Good, well I really am sorry.

Ruth: Right, well don't do it again. [At this point my then seven year old daughter walked off into the kitchen!]

SUMO pit stop

- Who do you know who would benefit from a good listening-to?

- What's your attitude like towards that person?

- How will you deal with distractions?

- What message are you sending this person when you *choose* to listen?

- When, where and with whom do you need to Listen Loud?

Small changes can bring high rewards.

SUMO
wisdom

Your SUMO takeaway

Listening is a vitally important skill if we're to build better relationships with others. Often our desire to 'strangle' someone stems from their unwillingness to listen to us and the frustration we feel as a result. However people may be more willing to listen to us if they feel we've listened to them.

What can hinder Listening Loud?

- Biology (we think faster than people can speak);

- Attitude (towards the other person); and

- Distraction.

To Listen Loud, remember:

- It's your choice.

- Put on a show – show that you're listening.

- Play detective – ask questions.

- State their case – summarise your understanding.

Shut Up lousy listening.
Move On to listening loud.

SUMO
wisdom

My SUMO takeaway from 'Listen Loud' is ...

S.U.M.O. TAKEAWAY

The Hijacker

Why you may want to strangle a hijacker

I love to talk. Those who know me will at this point nod their head in a very enthusiastic (and in my opinion slightly exaggerated) way.

Hijackers, though, don't just love to talk, they love to interrupt. Their mantra seems to be 'You've started, but I won't let you finish.' Their brains are hard-wired so that, whatever they hear someone else talking about, they'll bring the conversation back to themselves.

To an extent we all do it. Human interaction involves engaging with others by sharing your story and experiences.

Hijackers, however, have the ability to consistently and perhaps unknowingly do this. If there isn't a part of the conversation that they can hijack, they'd rather not interact at all – they'll just remain quiet until a topic arises that they can hijack by talking about their own experience.

A hijacker's definition of listening: *Pausing whilst I think of something else to say*.

Rather than engage in the other person's conversation by trying to understand their perspective, they simply want to manipulate the conversation so that they take centre stage. This is the most common type of hijacker – they're what I call the 'I can top that' hijacker.

However, there are two other 'varieties' of hijackers. There is the 'problem-solving hijacker'. They take over a conversation concerning a problem by providing a solution – usually before the other person has finished explaining the issue and, more importantly, how they feel about it. This trait seems particularly common amongst the male population. The third variety is the 'mind-reading hijacker' – they have the rather annoying habit of finishing off your sentences – often incorrectly. Unfortunately they're not very good mind-readers.

An 'I can top that' hijacker in conversation

You: I've had an awful weekend.

Hijacker: Wait till you hear about mine.

You: It took five hours to get to London by train on Sunday.

Hijacker: That's nothing. I once went to Scotland and it took 14 hours ... and my friend Kim, when she went to Lanzarote, the plane was delayed for three days. She was only going for a week.

You: Really? Well anyway I can't believe what a busy week I've got ahead of me.

Hijacker: Me too. I can't believe how much work they've given me.

You: Well, I've got two meetings already booked in for this morning.

Hijacker: Wait till you see my diary – the only blank space I've got is Sunday and I'll probably be catching up with admin. I don't think I've ever been so busy.

A 'problem-solving' hijacker' in conversation

You: I'm a bit worried. We never have time for each other any more. When was the last time we went out as a couple?

Hijacker: I'll take you to the pictures tomorrow. Now where's the remote control? The football starts in five minutes.

You: And the kids aren't well at the moment. I didn't get into work on time today because Karl was sick this morning and the traffic was awful.

Hijacker: Well I'd avoid Chester Road tomorrow – it's a nightmare there at the moment. And Karl needs an early night, that should sort him.

As far as the problem-solving hijacker is concerned, the problems are now resolved. Their goal when they hear about an issue is, 'How can I resolve this?' and not, 'Let me understand this'.

And finally …

A 'mind-reading' hijacker in conversation

You: You'll never guess what happened in the staff room at lunch. Terry only …

Hijacker: Dished the dirt on Louise?

You: No, he told us how at the team building weekend …

Hijacker: They spent three hours in the middle of a lake 'cos they couldn't decide how to build a bridge out of toilet rolls.

You: No. Terry was saying that on the weekend away, Clive had a right go at …

Hijacker: John. Yes I heard.

You: (A little more exasperated) No, not John.

Hijacker: Not John? Then who?

You: I'll tell you if you'll let me finish.

Hijacker: Sorry.

You: He said Clive had a go at Sam because she …

Hijacker: Messed up over the room bookings.

You: No. No. No! It had nothing to do with any room bookings. Clive had a go at Sam because in the team meetings Sam kept ...

Hijacker: Interrupting?

You: Yes. How did you know?

Hijacker: They don't call me a mind reader for nothing you know.

The impact of a hijacker

To perform effectively as human beings, we need to have a number of physical needs met. Food, water and exercise will all contribute to meeting these needs.

We also have a number of psychological and emotional needs. When our physical needs are not met, the consequences quickly become clear. When our psychological and emotional needs aren't met, the consequences can also be damaging. (An extreme example would be certain orphanages around the world where a child may be fed, but due to a lack of touch, mental stimulation or affection, starts to exhibit disturbing behaviour.)

Now a hijacker is unlikely to trigger such an extreme reaction (although there is one guy I know who, if he finishes off one of my sentences again, I'm likely to head-butt ... well, in my mind anyway!). But they can cause frustration in other people.

Two of our psychological needs are as follows. We want to feel **important** and we want to feel **understood**. When we're hijacked by another person, neither of these needs is being met. Consequently, we don't feel valued. When this occasionally happens or when you're talking about something relatively trivial, then the impact is minimal.

However, what about when it consistently happens and the hijacker is a key person in your life? What if you're hijacked by a person when you're in desperate need of Hippo Time?

Being regularly hijacked damages relationships. It prevents the development of depth and intimacy in our conversations. Dialogue becomes superficial and one-sided. We end up not communicating with them and withdrawing. The hijacker might not understand why, and the relationship can become very superficial or over-polite.

SUMO pit stop

- Recognise yourself in any of the previous descriptions?

- Think about your key relationships. How often are you likely to hijack?

- At work, how often is a team meeting hijacked by someone?

- If your partner has a problem they want to discuss, how good are you at really listening?

- Do you ever hijack your children? Do you give them a good listening to or do they rarely have an opportunity to have their say and explain how they're feeling?

The hijacker's side of the beachball

I'll be honest, listening to other people can be difficult. I don't find it easy to concentrate and to really focus on what the other person is saying. But when I start sharing my story, particularly one that relates to yours, that's my way of creating a mutual bond between us. As you're speaking, your conversation triggers off a thought in my mind which I want to share with you straight away. If I don't, I'll forget it.

Providing solutions to your problems is my way of being helpful. I guess I interpret the reason you're telling me your problem as you wanting a solution. I don't always realise that you might just want to be listened to. And when I finish off your sentences, at least I'm indicating that I am listening to what you're saying and am engaged in the conversation.

Can it ever be helpful to be a hijacker?

Occasionally yes. When someone is dominating a meeting or another person's ramblings leaves you gasping for breath in a sea of waffle then it might be appropriate to play the role of hijacker in order to gain some control or focus.

How to handle not strangle a hijacker

- Use the Magnus Magnusson approach (the guy who used to host the TV programme *Mastermind*). If he had started a question before the time was up, he'd say, 'I've started so I'll finish.' Don't be a victim to a hijacker. Whether it's in a team meeting or at home with your partner, be more assertive. Use phrases such as, 'I've not finished yet' or, 'If I could just finish my point'.

- Be a positive role model. When you catch yourself 'hijacking' at an inappropriate time, apologise to the other person, 'Sorry I interrupted you. You were saying?' By doing this, the other person might become more aware that they do the same.

- Communicate your needs. If you simply want to talk through an issue or are in need of Hippo Time, let the other person know what you want or don't want from them **before** you start talking. For example, 'Look, I just want to talk this through, please don't give me any answers, I just want you to listen.'

- If you believe you're regularly being hijacked, ask for some feedback. Do people feel the need to do this because you have a tendency to waffle and take ages to get to your point? Do you lack sensitivity to the needs of others and take too long talking when time is short?

• Show a little compassion. Remember most hijackers are unaware of what they are doing and the potential negative impact they're having on you.

When a hijacker says ...	You might want to say ...
The same thing happened to me ...	Really? I'd love to hear about it, but is it OK if I just finish my point?
Well you know what you should have done ...	There's lots I'm sure I could have done, but can I just tell you how I'm feeling at the moment?
Well if I was you ...	Thanks for that suggestion but what I really need at the moment is someone to listen whilst I get things off my chest.
I bet I know what happened next ...	Well if you're correct I'll let you know – if not, you owe me a drink!

Handling the hijacker in yourself

1   **Shut Up** always bringing the conversation back to your own experience.

   Move On to allowing others centre stage.

2   **Shut Up** talking.

   Move On to Listening Loud.

3   **Shut Up** trying to solve people's problems.

Move On trying to understand people's issues.

4   **Shut Up** trying to anticipate what others will say.

Move on to allowing people time to talk.

SUMO pit stop

If you relate to some or all of the hijackers' behaviour then you may need to re-visit the SUMO Insight 'Listen Loud' or, if you're brave enough and you know a hijacker, get them to read it.

Excel In Encouragement

When you talk to people, how many do you know who say, 'My problem is I've had too many people encouraging me.' Not many? Me neither. The dictionary uses the following words to define the word 'encourage':

> **Encourage** – *give courage, stimulate by help, reward, assist, advise.*
> *It literally means – 'to put courage into someone'.*

As a way of developing great relationships, it's like an essential ingredient. Here's another way of thinking about the power of encouragement. Think of words to describe 'discouragement' and its affects on people. Ones that come to mind for me include:

- fear;

- lack of confidence;

- obstruction;

- hinderance; and

- lack of support.

So here's the reality: relationships both in and outside the workplace will suffer when there's a deficit of encouragement. (I'm using the word 'encourage' in the context of achieving a positive outcome for both ourselves and others.)

The personal stuff

Academically, I would not describe myself as the brightest lad in the class. Mathematics was a constant struggle, foreign languages were a mystery and I probably still hold the school record for the lowest marks ever achieved in a Physics exam. Despite this, I did enjoy English and History and scraped by in some other subjects. By age sixteen, I was sitting my 'O' levels (now referred to in Britain as GCSE exams). I passed five in total. (It would have been six, but my clay pot blew up in the kiln, thus thwarting my attempt to achieve a pass in Pottery.)

No one in my family had achieved such dizzy academic heights before and although she was in no way deluded by my success, my mum was obviously proud of her son. (Before progressing, readers need to be aware that 5 'O' levels in 1980 is probably the equivalent of 28 today ... plus a PhD.)

I just about managed to get into the sixth form to do my 'A' levels, although, perhaps not surprisingly, Physics and Pottery were not two of my chosen subjects. Deep down, I felt I had probably reached the pinnacle of my educational achievements and although I hoped to pass my 'A' levels, further education beyond these exams was not on my horizon.

To the best of my knowledge, I was the only pupil in my class who was not considering applying to university or polytechnic after my exams. My dream was to become an actor or a journalist, although I actually had a job lined up as a bank clerk. Why? It's a long story.

Then, after a particularly enjoyable English lesson, a thought came to mind. Maybe I'm not clever enough academically to go to university (a destination that seemed as realistic then as the England football team winning a penalty shoot out does now), but what about polytechnic? The grades typically required to go there were not as high. I felt buoyed by my own sense of rising self-belief. I felt good about myself. I felt positive about the future.

In less than a minute, those feelings had changed. As I walked down the school corridor, I saw one of the heads of the sixth form walking towards me. I was keen to share my new academic goal.

Me: Sir, can I have a quick word?

Teacher: Yes.

Me: Sir ... er ... obviously I'm not good enough to go to university. [I've always been an expert in false humility.]

Teacher: Yes. [Nodding his head with just a little too much enthusiasm for my liking.]

Me: Well Sir, I was wondering. Do you think I should apply for poly-technic?

Teacher: Haven't you got a job lined up in the bank?

Me: Er ... yes Sir, I have. [Trying to remain composed as I sensed my newly built wall of confidence beginning to crumble before me.]

Teacher: [Now making eye contact for the first time during our brief conversation.] Well if I were you ... I'd stick with that.

He paused, presumably waiting for a response. I said nothing. I thought to myself 'How stupid do I feel?'

Teacher: Was there anything else?

Me: Er, no Sir, that's fine ... er ... like you say, best stick with what I already have.

The conversation lasted less than a minute.

It influenced what I did with the next 12 months of my life.

I didn't apply to university or polytechnic. I joined the bank. I hated it. Six weeks after joining, I received my 'A' level results. They were good enough for me to go to university.

Words, wonderful words

Ancient scripture says words have the power to bring life or death. Whoever wrote that, I agree. Yet, as a kid, I learnt the following rhyme:

'Sticks and stones may break my bones
But words will never hurt me'

That's wrong. Very wrong. Words can inspire or kill a dream. They can build or destroy a child's confidence. They can motivate or demoralise a workforce. Sometimes, it's not even what is said. It's simply the silence. The lack of approval. The lack of support. The lack of encouragement. Perhaps the words of a poem by Barrie Wade are more appropriate:

Sticks and stones may break my bones,
But words can also hurt me.
Stones and sticks break only skin
While words are ghosts that haunt me.

In the workplace, it's easy for managers to fall into the trap of believing that too much encouragement can breed complacency. I think this can happen if we see the meaning of encouragement as only ever giving praise and positive feedback. To me, encouragement is so much more.

Yes, it is about thanking people for their contribution and appreciating them for who they are, rather than simply for what they do. But it's also about challenging people. It's making them aware of the potential you see in them and helping them to reach higher in order to achieve it.

The work stuff

It's January 1995 and I was just starting out in my career as a speaker. I'm presenting my first ever business seminar for a new client. They often run highly motivational sessions on topics related to customer service and excelling as a team. The topic I'm presenting is rather less exciting … certainly the title is anyway: 'How to Discipline Employees and Correct Performance Problems'.

In order to inject a little light relief into the day, I decided to use a little humour. (Well I thought it was humorous anyway.) After a brief introduction, I set the scene in the following way:

'Ladies and gentlemen, there are only four things you can do with a difficult employee. Firstly you can choose to ignore them and hope they either improve or perhaps leave. Secondly you can coach or counsel them in the hope their performance will improve. Thirdly you can take them down the disciplinary route, which may ultimately lead to dismissal. Finally you can shoot them. So out of those four approaches, which one will we focus on initially? Well let's start with the last one. We'll be exploring just what kind of gun to use …'

I sense that, as you read these words, you're not laughing. Neither was my audience. It was a disastrous start to my new career. I battled through the rest of the day. It was a heavy topic and they were a serious audience. The day ended and the audience left. I was not looking forward to reading the evaluation forms. I squirmed at some of the comments. A few were more encouraging.

Jacqueline Guthrie had sat at the back of the room throughout the day. She worked for the seminar company I was representing. She had been responsible for recruiting me and was there to assess me. We grabbed a coffee and a quiet table. We talked for two hours. So much of what she said was helpful and constructive, but there was one sentence she said that I will always remember.

'Paul, today was not a roaring success and for your very first presentation, I didn't expect it to be. But I saw enough today to make me believe you have the potential to be one of our top presenters.'

I was the youngest presenter they had ever used in the UK. Jacqueline's words brought a feeling of both relief and pride. I had a long way to go, but her encouragement had fanned the flames of my self belief.

What stops us encouraging more often?

I think there are several reasons:

1   *We think people don't actually need it.* Young children may
    need some encouragement but, once they've learnt to
    walk and talk, there's no perceived need for it any more.

2   *We're not actually sure how to go about it.* We feel uncomfort-
    able about how and when to encourage others.

3   *People may question our motives when we seek to encourage
    them* ... particularly if it's not part of our normal behaviour.
    We believe they'll think we've either been on a course
    or are trying to get in their good books because we want
    them to do something for us.

4   *Our encouragement may be rejected.* Sometimes people brush
    off our encouragement by saying things like, 'Oh it was
    nothing', and so we begin to question the point of trying
    to encourage others.

The truth, of course, is that encouragement can be incredibly
powerful in helping and inspiring others, and our focus should
not be on the reasons why we don't do it, but on deciding to
make it a habit in how we deal with others.

SUMO
wisdom

Shut Up making excuses.
Move On to excelling in encouragement.

So what can you do to encourage others?

1   **Make being an encourager a habit** rather than simply a technique to use when you want to see performance (at work) or behaviour (at home) improve. Recognise it's a great quality. Period. You might not always see instant results, but that's not your motive. Being someone who encourages others becomes one of your character traits.

2   **Thank people**. Obvious? Yes. So tell me how often have you done it today? Did you make eye contact when you did it? Did you smile? Did you touch the other person? (Before you suggest I'm advising you to do something that could lead to you being accused of sexual harassment, I suggest this is likely to be more appropriate in your personal life.)

3   **Be creative**. If you or the other person is uncomfortable with face to face encouragement, then one of the following may help:

   • Send a text message.
   • Send an email.
   • Write a letter.
   • Send a card. (You could even send an e-card. Go to www. TheSumoGuy.com for a few ideas.)
   • Buy a gift. This doesn't need to be expensive, just thoughtful. A friend of mine recently bought me a couple of personalised identification straps for my luggage. Not only does it make my luggage easier to identify, but I'll think of them every time I travel.

4   **Pass on praise**. Perhaps it's from a customer, a colleague or a teacher. Make the praise or positive feedback the focal point of your communication rather than simply a passing comment.

5   **Make time for feedback**. People like to know where they stand. Feedback gives you an opportunity to communicate your perceptions of others. Even pointing out 'areas for development' can be encouraging. When people know what they're doing right and where they need to improve, this in itself can be motivating.

SUMO wisdom

When it comes to encouraging others, silence is rarely golden.

6   **Challenge people.** Complacency is a trap that people can easily fall into. So set new goals and fresh targets and raise the bar in terms of what you expect of others. If people already feel valued, this new challenge encourages them to raise their sights higher. It also sends a powerful message about the belief you have in their potential.

7   **Recognise progress and effort.** If we only praise and encourage our 'stars', then we automatically disqualify others. We may need to encourage people at times to simply 'hang on in there', and not to give up in the face of obstacles and setbacks. Encourage the progress people make rather than waiting for perfection to be achieved before you recognise their efforts.

The work stuff

Having been involved in a voluntary capacity with an organisation looking to find a new full-time worker, I sent the following email to one of the committee:

'Hi Dave, just putting together a newsletter that I'm sending to clients about the importance of giving people credit who are often the unseen people involved with a task. It made me realise how much you do in relation to finding John's replacement. I simply turn up to the meetings and say a few words – you do so much more. So I wanted to say I do appreciate all you're doing and realise how much it helps the process of finding a new worker. Cheers, Paul.'

And Dave's reply:

'Paul, That's very kind of you. I like to think of myself as performing best as a team player and I'm very happy in that role. Consequently I don't expect to receive praise as a rule. I'm not comfortable in the limelight, however it's nice to receive some unsought appreciation from time to time – it does the self-esteem a world of good – so thank you.

'Regards, Dave.'

SUMO pit stop

- Review the previous seven points on ways to encourage others.

- Which strategy will you use today to encourage someone?

- Which do you tend to use already?

Now here's something that really discourages people ...

When others take your credit

Perhaps one of the most discouraging times for a person is when, after all their hard work, someone else takes their credit. The following humorous example illustrates how this can happen.

The barbeque season is always an interesting time in the UK. Often it's the only type of cooking a 'real' man will do (probably because there is an element of danger involved). When a man volunteers to do the BBQ, the following chain of events are put into motion:

Routine:
1 The woman buys the food.
2 The woman makes the salad, prepares the vegetables and makes dessert.
3 The woman prepares the meat for cooking, places it on a tray along with the necessary cooking utensils and sauces and takes it to the man who is lounging beside the grill, beer in hand.

Here comes the important part:
4 **The man places the meat on the BBQ.**

More routine:
5 The woman goes inside to organise the plates and cutlery.
6 The woman comes out to tell the man that the meat is burning. He thanks her and asks if she will bring another beer while he deals with the situation.

Important again:
7 **The man takes the meat off the BBQ and hands it to the woman.**

More routine:
8 The woman prepares the plates, salad, bread, utensils, napkins and sauces and brings them to the table.
9 After eating, the woman clears the table and does the dishes.

And most important of all:
10 **Everyone praises the man and thanks him for his cooking efforts.**
11. The man asks the woman how she enjoyed 'her night off'. And, upon seeing her annoyed reaction, he concludes that there's just no pleasing some women ...

SUMO wisdom

Shut Up taking all the credit.
Move On to spreading the praise.

And here's an example of how not everyone has quite mastered the art of encouragement ...

The work stuff

I had been presenting a seminar on delivering superior service, and emphasised the importance of how each member of staff makes a difference. At the end of the day, three women from the same organisation approached me. The conversation went something like this:

Me: Hi folks, did you enjoy the day?

Women: Great thanks. We all found it very useful. But we've got a question.

Me: OK, fire away.

Women: We've got a member of staff who we don't feel is performing as well as they could do. We've tried everything but nothing seems to work. What do you suggest?

Me: When you say you've tried everything, what exactly have you done?

Women: Well we tried the obvious.

Me: The obvious?

Women: Yeah, we've tried humiliating them.

Me: Humiliating them?

Women: Yeah and to be honest that didn't work as well as we expected.

Me: Really? [Whilst my jaw gently caressed the floor.]

SUMO pit stop

- Is there anyone in your world who is suffering through a lack of encouragement?

- Could this be one reason why their relationships with others are not as they could be?

- If you feel you need some encouragement, perhaps you need to express your expectations.

SUMO wisdom

Resentment grows through a lack of encouragement.

SUMO takeaway

Setbacks and disappointments are part of life. Coupled with this fact is our tendency as human beings to focus on where people make mistakes and fall short. Such scenarios can lead to discouragement and demotivation to those on the receiving end.

Encouraging people can be relatively easy to do – it's also easy not to do. Your words to a colleague, friend or child can have a huge impact. Your encouragement can literally influence people's destiny. Those who felt like giving up may try one more time because of what you say and do. Those who were ready to quit their job may stay and those that felt they were making little difference in life may rediscover their self-belief.

The art of encouragement … it's not a technique, it's a way of life.

My SUMO takeaway from 'Excel in Encouragement' is ...

S.U.M.O. TAKEAWAY

The Awfuliser

Why you may want to strangle an awfuliser

There was once an advert shown in Britain where the organisation's catch phrase was, 'We won't turn a drama into a crisis.'

An awfuliser would beg to differ. For them, the phrase, 'We'll turn the ordinary into the awful' is more appropriate. With great skill and enthusiasm, they can take a minor setback and turn it into a crisis. Awfulisers draw attention to the downside of situations … 'never forget, every silver lining has a black cloud.' They tend to lay on the empathy and sympathy a little too thick and their favourite phrase, not surprisingly is; 'That's awful.'

An awfuliser in conversation in the workplace

You: Business is slow at the moment.

Awfuliser: They reckon there's a recession on the way. I knew the good times wouldn't last long.

You: But I've a few irons in the fire though.

Awfuliser: Yes, but how many of them will come to anything? Do you think you'll lose your job?

You: Well I don't think things are quite that bad.

Awfuliser: Clare, my friend, was made redundant a few months back and she's still out of work now. She seems to have lost all motivation and it's been a real kick in the teeth, particularly at her age.

You: But Clare's younger than me.

Awfuliser: That's what I mean. Once you lose your job, it won't be easy getting another one. But hey, if that happens, you know where I am if you need me. That's when you discover who your friends are.

You: Right. Well, that's … er … really reassuring to know.

An awfuliser in conversation outside the workplace

You: I'm thinking of trying to lose some weight.

Awfuliser: It won't be easy you know – not at your age.

You: What's my age got to do with it?

Awfuliser: Your metabolism slows down. It's even harder to lose weight now you've passed forty.

You: Well I'm going to do some exercise as well – that should help.

Awfuliser: Gym membership is very pricey though. Can you afford it?

You: I was thinking of taking up jogging.

Awfuliser: Jogging? At this time of year?

You: What's wrong with this time of year or any other for that matter?

Awfuliser: It's the dark winter nights – you don't seriously want to be pounding the streets in darkness do you?

You: Other people do it. Anyway I'm determined to lose some weight. I've even go a new motto 'Lose the Lard.'

Awfuliser: Well I think you're being silly – don't you read the papers?

You: What do you mean?

Awfuliser: There was a jogger killed last week by a hit and run driver. He had a wife and four children. He was only thirty four.

You: Have you ever thought of a career as a motivational speaker?

Awfuliser: Look, I'm only trying to be helpful. Anyway, do you fancy some chocolate – I've got a couple of bars in the cupboard.

The impact of an awfuliser

Awfulisers can have good intentions. They are not necessarily sad or miserable in nature. But – and it's a big but – they seem to have a morbid fascination with bad news. And when you do have some bad news, you're probably best off avoiding them.

The phrase 'a trouble shared is a trouble halved' does not apply when you're sharing your news with this character – it's more a case of 'double your trouble'. In fact, it's possible that you could walk into a room with a problem, meet the awfuliser, share your news – and then leave with depression. They have the ability to escalate the seriousness of issues and, in doing so, they can leave you feeling less confident and able to deal with your challenges.

> **SUMO wisdom**
>
> When you're having Hippo Time avoid awfulisers at all costs – that's unless you're committed to wallowing long term.

The awfuliser might not be the first person to identify a problem, but when someone does, it triggers a reaction and they begin to feed upon this scrap of bad news. Five minutes later they've turned it into a five-course meal. If you're in Hippo Time, rationally speaking, you may have concluded that, on a scale of 1–10 (where ten equates to death), your problem registers a three. If you then share your news with an awfuliser, you start to believe it could actually be a seven or even an eight.

The song *You'll never walk alone* by Gerry and The Pacemakers, includes the words, 'with hope in your hearts'. With awfulisers, there seems there is no hope – just a fresh appreciation of a problem that you'd failed to notice before.

The personal stuff

I joined the Professional Speakers Association as a founder member in 1999. I spoke at their first conference a year later. My talk went well and I thought I was finally on the verge of breaking through as a speaker. The feedback I received was positive. But then I chatted with Janice. Janice worked with speakers and helped them to find work. Within five minutes of speaking to Janice I felt ready to quit the speaking profession. She gave me a reality check. She pointed out that it was extremely difficult for a non-celebrity person like myself to break through into the competitive world of business and motivational speaking.

'You've not climbed Everest, won a gold medal or earned a million pounds by the time you're twenty five', she explained. 'Most agents who promote speakers won't want to know you. You don't stand out enough.'

She then elaborated on how one now very successful speaker had lost his leg through a land mine accident and also been held hostage by a group of rebel fighters in Cambodia. He was very popular with his audiences, apparently.

I reflected on what she said. My talk included a story about how I struggled to go shopping in a supermarket with two young children on a Saturday morning. I have both my legs. Janice wasn't simply giving me a reality check, she was draining me of hope. Awfulisers do that. I'm sure they don't mean to, but they do.

The awfuliser's side of the beachball

When you've got a problem, come to me. I will listen. I won't trivialise your issue. I won't dismiss you as being silly. I will empathise. That's what you want, isn't it? I will take what you say seriously. I'll even point out – in a helpful way, of course – some factors of your problem that you might not even have considered. When you want to get things off your chest, I'll be there for you. I'll support you. I'll work hard at understanding how bad you feel. You can count on me. And if you want the truth about things, I'll tell you the truth. I won't patronise you by putting a positive slant on what I know are serious issues. Do you understand where I'm coming from?

SUMO pit stop

Have you ever felt drawn to an awfuliser because you actually *wanted to feel worse about a situation?*

SUMO wisdom

For some people their way of connecting with others is through adversity.

Can it ever be helpful to be an awfuliser?

Rarely. However there may be an occasion when something of importance is not being taken seriously by others – an issue around health and safety comes to mind. Perhaps the awfuliser's approach might be needed then in order to jolt people out of their pit of complacency.

How to handle not strangle an awfuliser

- Draw out the awfuliser's comments into the open. Acknowledge them and then deal with their points. Be prepared to ask questions. For example:

When an awfuliser says …	You might want to say …
I'm not sure this is going to work out as planned.	OK, so what's the worst that can happen here? (Awfulisers immediately think Christmas has arrived.) Then you follow up on their comments with further questions: 1 So how realistic is that scenario? (Challenges people's perception of reality.) **OR** 2 What actions can we take to influence or improve the situation? (Focuses people on the solution rather than the problem.) **OR** 3 What can we find that's positive in the situation? (Helps people put things into perspective and look for the up-side without ignoring the down-side.)
You must be really struggling at the moment.	You're right, it's not been easy, but I'm aware how I'm feeling now won't last for ever.
This is a major setback.	It's certainly a setback and we need some Hippo Time, but I think we're also going to have to focus on how we'll bounce back.

You need to bring issues out into the open before you can help move people on.

SUMO wisdom

- If you're dealing with an awfuliser outside a work context, you need to seriously decide whether or not to share your problems with them. Are you emotionally resilient enough to handle their response? Are you out of your own Hippo Time yet? Often when an awfuliser asks about your situation it's best to keep things brief. You might reply, 'Well I've known things to be better, but let's not go there.' And then quickly change the subject.

• Sometimes though, you want to talk and at least the awfuliser gives you time to do so. What's the best approach then? Be up-front before you start talking. For example:

> *'Look, before I share this with you, I want you to know I'll be OK. I am upset, but I'm also aware that what seems like a huge issue now, won't be in six months' time. I appreciate your interest and I want you to understand that I want you to help me move on from this.'*

• If your organisation is facing challenges, recognise that people need Hippo Time and a chance to air their fears and concerns. When an awfuliser expresses their views, it could deflate everybody. So it's important to challenge their comments. If they remain unchecked, it's their words, not yours, that others will remember.

Handling the awfuliser in yourself

1   **Shut Up** developing your reputation as a doom and gloom merchant.

    Move On to giving people some hope and help.

2   **Shut Up** being unaware of the impact your behaviour has on others.

    Move On to being more conscious of the impact you're making.

3   **Shut Up** making mountains out of mole-hills.

    Move On to bringing perspective and possible solutions.

SUMO pit stop

- Who are the awfulisers in your life?

- How can you limit the impact they have on you and those around them?

- Do you ever exhibit awfuliser tendencies? How can you ensure that empathising doesn't lead to awfulising?

Express Your Expectations

I recently heard the following story from a former head teacher. When she was marking her 'A' level students' essays, she would approach the person who, in her opinion, had written the most effective essay and ask for their permission to photocopy it. The essay was then distributed to the other students in her class.

Her reason?

She wanted the other students to know her expectations when it came to writing an economics essay. 'I want them to know what someone has to do in order to get a top mark. If I don't show them, how will they know? What's the point of asking them to try harder if they're not sure what trying harder leads to?'

It was a brilliant example of letting others be clear on what you expect. But, in my experience, when it comes to relationships, we don't always make our expectations clear. Let's explore a couple of reasons why.

1 Away with your assumptions

I guess many of us assume others know what our expectations are. In many cases, we'd be right. I have a range of expectations when I go out for a meal – prompt service, clean cutlery, tasty food, etc. I might not always have these expectations met, but they would not be considered unrealistic or unfair. Our challenge comes when we assume people can clearly see how things look from our side of the beachball – when in fact they don't. And when what we perceive as very obvious and clear expectations are not being met, then, inevitably, conflict will arise.

It's a very well used illustration, but still one worth repeating – when you break the word 'assume' down into three sections, it becomes 'ass u me'. Often when you assume something, you can make an *ass* out of *u* and *me*.

2 But I shouldn't have to tell you

For the first few years of our marriage, 'But I shouldn't have to tell you', was Helen's most common phrase to me. However, her expectation that I was a fully 'switched-on' male who constantly looked around the house for things to do was grossly misplaced. We had some interesting conversations.

Eventually the penny dropped and we changed our communication strategy. We ditched our assumptions and decided there were times when we both needed to clearly communicate our needs and expectations.

It's an approach which is critical not just in the home but also in the workplace.

We can make certain assumptions about the people we work with and how we expect them to behave. You may have a view on how a boss should treat their staff, how colleagues should interact with each other and how customers should treat their suppliers. However, people's behaviour is influenced by their values and their upbringing, and what would seem a natural and normal response to one person could seem quite alien to another.

When we assume others know what we want, what we're thinking and how we want to be treated, we'll often be disappointed. But if we simply blame the other person and state, 'I shouldn't have to tell you', we fail to take responsibility for expressing our own needs.

SUMO wisdom

If your expectations aren't being met, It's easy to wear the victim T-shirt and play the blame game. There are no winners in the blame game.

SUMO pit stop

- Who do you need to clearly express your expectations to? (A partner? A manager? A colleague? A customer? A child?)

- Are you clear on what your expectations are?

- What conversation needs to take place that currently isn't happening?

- When could that conversation take place?

- Remember we are responsible for ensuring that people understand what we require or how we feel. Take the guesswork out of your relationships – express your expectations.

The work stuff

I used to work with an American organisation presenting their one-day seminars throughout the UK. I was assisted at the various locations by someone known as the Programme Manager. Their role was to meet and greet delegates as they arrived, register them and deal with any queries they may have. They were also involved in the promoting of additional training resources such as CDs and DVDs for people to purchase.

In short, although delegates would spend most of the day listening to me, the role of the Programme Manager was very important. When, due to illness, a Programme Manager wasn't available, they were replaced by temporary staff from a local agency. On one such occasion Mike, who was in his early twenties, worked with me. He had already been briefed that a smart appearance (shirt and tie) were essential and that he'd need to present a polite and professional image at all times. Well, he was wearing a shirt and tie – the tie was loosely fitted, the shirt was un-ironed, and his hair looked like it had been some time since it was last acquainted with a comb.

We had a chat. From his perspective, this was simply a one-day agency job and his main aim was to see out the day, avoid boredom and collect his money.

I made my expectations very clear. Today he wasn't to see himself as 'just agency staff', but as an ambassador of an organisation. I informed him that he had a part to play in how successful the day would be, that delegates had an evaluation form and some would write comments about him. I spelt out that I needed his support and that we would need to work as a team. Finally I told him that the first impression he created when people arrived would set the tone of the day.

Thirty minutes later, Mike's attitude and appearance were somewhat different.

We had a great day.

Rather than moan about the agency and the type of person they'd sent me, I found spelling out my expectations, and the reasons for them, got the desired result.

Communicating your own expectations within a relationship is essential, but so too is understanding the expectations of others. Let's look at this in more detail.

Understand others' expectations

Any successful relationship is based upon two-way communication – so it's crucial that we allow others the time and opportunity to communicate their expectations to us. So in the workplace, employees need the opportunity to discuss not just their performance at work, but also how satisfied they are in what they're doing and also what their own expectations regarding the job are. Great questions for a manager to ask their staff would include:

- 'Is this job what you expected it to be? If not, how can we develop your role?'

- 'Is there anything you would expect from a manager that I'm not currently providing?'

- 'How could I help you more?'

If you need to communicate your expectations to your boss, you might ask:

- 'Can we discuss what would really help me in my role working for you?'

This could create the platform for you to discuss in more detail your own expectations and also possible concerns.

But it's not just in the workplace where it's important for people to talk about their expectations. I find it's important to do in family relationships.

The personal stuff

A glorious hot day in September – a rare occurrence in the UK. (OK I admit it, I'm slipping into awfuliser mode). As a family, we were enjoying Sunday lunch in the garden, eating our traditional Sunday fayre. When I say traditional, I mean in the 'McGee family' sense. We all eagerly tucked into, not a leg of lamb, joint of beef or some delicious roast chicken, but into whatever happened to be in the fridge at the time ... cottage cheese, cold baked beans, overripe cucumber – we had it all.

A small cardboard box was in the garden and Ruth used it as a bin for her leftovers. I reminded her to empty the box and dispose of it in the main dustbin. A few minutes later, a friend of hers arrived and she dashed into the house, leaving the box in the garden. As we were in a hurry to get out and visit some friends, I asked Matt to help with the clearing up, including Ruth's leftovers. He did so, but in a way that gave the impression he was not particularly pleased.

Later that evening I was discussing this chapter of the book with Helen. Matt was also around and I mentioned that I feel it's appropriate at times for children to have the opportunity to communicate their expectations to their parents in relation to how they're treated. (I recognise a level of maturity is required from both parties in order to do this and, I confess, it's not something we have done on a regular basis.)

Matt seized his opportunity. 'In that case Dad, I want you to know I wasn't happy having to clear up after Ruth this lunchtime. You asked her to clear up, she didn't and you got me to do it instead.'

I explained to Matt we were in a hurry and let's not make a big issue out of it.

'That's fine Dad. Next time you ask me to do something and I don't, you can always get Ruth to clear up after me then.'

He was assertive but calm.

I felt he had a point.

He wasn't too bothered about putting stuff in the bin, just the inconsistency of my approach – specifically asking Ruth to do something and then turning to him when she didn't do it. He communicated his expectations and I apologised.

And that's when our previous Sumo Insight 'Humility Helps' becomes so important. We have to be humble enough to admit there are times when we haven't met the expectations of others and we need to admit our mistake and apologise.

SUMO pit stop

If you have children, would you ever consider it appropriate to find out their expectations of you?

OK, so up until now we've looked at the reasons why failing to express our expectations can lead to conflict and also the importance of understanding the expectations of others. Now onto another important factor when it comes to expectations.

Have realistic expectations

Communicating your expectations is one thing, but it's useful to question how realistic they are. When I think about my expectations concerning my relationships with people in and outside the workplace; **ideally** I'd like the following to happen.

At work

- All the work I bid for to be successfully won.

- All clients to return my phone calls promptly – preferably within thirty minutes.

- All delegates to appreciate my sense of humour and laugh without inhibition.

- All clients to pay promptly.

- All work to come my way without the need for any marketing.

- All road works to be postponed during the hours when I'm travelling to a venue.

- All flights to leave promptly when I'm flying.

At home

- Ruth to discover a fascination verging on obsession to tidy up after herself.

- Helen to always feel passionate and in the mood to satisfy her physical desires at the same times as me. (Sadly she's not often awake at 3 o'clock in the morning.)

- Helen to clearly see my rationale and logic over every decision I make and never question my actions.

- Matthew to realise that the 120-mile round trip to watch Bradford City is well worth his time and energy, and to appreciate the lessons that can be learnt from watching a third-rate football team and eating an overcooked balti pie at half time.

SUMO wisdom

Shut Up unrealistic expectations. Move On to the real world.

The work stuff

When I'm running a workshop, I'm always keen to manage my delegates' expectations and make sure they're realistic. I recognise that if I cover a topic they're familiar with, their approach can be to immediately switch off with the attitude, 'I've heard all this before.'

To overcome this, I start by explaining the three 'R's; **R**einforced, **R**eminded, **R**evealed. I explain how some of what we will explore will reinforce what they already know and do. I follow this with a question, 'But does Tiger Woods still practise his golf?'

Just because we're already good at something, it doesn't mean we can ignore a particular talent or ability.

Secondly, I elaborate on why it's important to be reminded of things.

It's one thing to have knowledge of a subject, but unless we review it regularly and apply what we know, our memories can quickly fade. In an age where we are constantly being bombarded with information, it's useful at times to be reminded of the basics. I then get the group's agreement that this is a valid point. Finally, I manage expectations by saying some of what we will explore may be new to them and they will gain new insights that they had not considered before.

Within the first few minutes of my relationship with the group, I'm seeking to manage expectations and therefore influence their attitude towards their learning experience. On occasions, I also might ask the group what they hope to gain from the session. In many cases, people have simply come along because they've been told to attend, but some people come with very specific expectations.

I once ran a workshop for an organisation on 'How to Influence and Persuade Others'. Gemma was 18 years old and relatively new to the organisation. I asked each delegate in turn what they hoped to gain from the session. When it came to Gemma, she'd obviously been rehearsing her answer, 'I'd like to feel totally confident and effective in being able to influence and persuade all groups of people, including the board of directors.' It was a one-day workshop. I admired her high expectations – but I also sought to manage them in terms of what she was likely to gain from our few hours together.

The personal stuff

It's unrealistic to spend the whole night breaking wind, burping and stuffing your face with food and then turn to your partner with a twinkle in your eye and ask, 'Do you fancy an early night?' – and expect a positive response.

SUMO pit stop

Are some of your relationship difficulties due to unrealistic expectations? Who holds those unrealistic expectations – you? The other party? Both of you?

Identify some specific expectations that on reflection may be unrealistic. What would be more realistic in those situations?

Express yourself

Let's get very practical. The following table illustrates three ways in which our expectations might not be being met and what we might consider doing as an alternative.

If your expectations are ...	You might want to consider ...
Unstated	Expressing what you want clearly; e.g. 'I would be happy to work late tonight, but I'd want to leave early on Friday. Is that OK?'
Unrealistic	Revising your expectations and deciding what actually is acceptable to you; e.g. 'I don't expect your bedroom to be spotless all the time but I do want you to hang up your school uniform at night.'
Unclear	Being more clear and direct; e.g. 'I realise I might not have made myself clear before, but I really would appreciate ...'

SUMO pit stop

- Think of a relationship where you feel you may have expectations that are unstated, unrealistic or unclear.

- What action do you need to take in order to either express, revise or clarify your expectations?

The personal stuff

Some of the greatest and most effective sales people I've ever met are children. My two are no exception, particularly Ruth. She wanted a dog. Our personal circumstances meant this was unrealistic. Ruth was wise enough to understand that no matter how much she persisted, the fact that there would be at least two days of the week when no one was at home meant it was unlikely to happen.

She changed her mind. She wanted a cat, or to be more specific, a kitten. Her goal then was to sell us on the idea of having one.

I don't like cats. I tried to sell Ruth on the delights of having our two goldfish. She still wanted a cat. After months of persistence on her part, we relented. We are now the owners of two adorable (did I just say 'adorable'?) kittens. However, before I agreed, I made my expectations very clear. When it comes to litter tray disposal, that's her job. In fact, failure to take responsibility for her new pets could lead to them being returned. Compassionate, aren't I? But Ruth is clear on where I stand and, perhaps more importantly, has agreed to my terms. (We set them out in an official document, similar to that of the Geneva Convention. We've had three copies made, one of which is with my solicitor.)

We've also taken steps to ensure that our new members of the family, Louis and Muffin are clear on our expectations in terms of where they can go and what they can do in our house. Our pump-action, sawn-off water pistol makes sure of that!

SUMO takeaway

1   It's easy to make assumptions that people know what our expectations are – they don't always.

2   Despite how well you might know someone, they are not mind-readers – so don't expect your unspoken words to be understood by others.

3   Take responsibility for expressing your expectations rather than playing the blame game.

4   Make sure you give time and opportunity for others to express their expectations.

5   Be flexible – have realistic expectations that can be achievably met – otherwise face up to continually being disappointed.

My SUMO takeaway from 'Express Your Expectations' is …

The Happy

Why you may want to strangle a happy

It might seem strange to include a character called a 'happy' in a book about improving relationships. Doesn't everyone want to be surrounded by happy people? I guess it all depends on your definition of 'happy'. In this context, a 'happy' is a person who is rarely in touch with reality. They seem unaware of how inappropriate and unhelpful their 'let's be positive' attitude can be to someone who's struggling.

Is there a place for a positive attitude? Of course there is. Most of the time in fact. But Happies can trivialise issues and fail to face up to the harsh reality of some situations. Their approach is often not solution-focused, but rather, 'Well let's think about something else.' Their behaviour can at times lack sensitivity and understanding and they can see problems as something to sweep under the carpet or dismiss with trite phrases such as, 'Never mind, everything will be alright.'

These can be reassuring words on occasions, but they can also create a false sense of security and discourage the tackling of issues. Their approach can be passive rather than productive

A happy in conversation in the workplace

You: I'm a little concerned about the lack of orders in the book for the next three months.

Happy: We'll be fine, something always crops up at the last minute.

You: I'm not so sure. The way things are developing in Europe at the moment, other companies can under-cut our prices.

Happy: Look, I just think you're worrying unnecessarily. The competition can't compete with us on service and they haven't got our expertise.

You: How do you know that? That's a big assumption to make.

Happy: Look, I'm confident the business will come. Don't start slipping into thinking negatively. Remember what the motivational speaker said, 'Always look on the bright side of life.'

You: Yes, I remember him alright. But I don't think we should look on the bright side and simply ignore the other side. I've got some real concerns.

Happy: OK, but I just think you should be more positive. I bet you this time next week, you'll be wondering why on earth you were so worried. Now, who's getting the coffee, you or me?

A happy in conversation outside the workplace

You: Terrible news about Frank and his accident. He lost both legs you know.

Happy: Yes I heard. Still, he's got both his arms.

You: I know, but even so, it's awful news.

Happy: It's amazing what these wheelchairs can do now though. And I guess he'll save a fortune in not having to buy shoes or socks.

You: You're heartless at times, you are.

Happy: Just trying to be positive. There's too much negativity in the world as it is. Anyway, how are you and Colin? Still seeing plenty of each other?

You: Actually we're not. He told me things were over between us last week.

Happy: I never did like him. He wasn't your sort. You're better off without him.

You: Hang on a minute, I thought you liked him. You told me you thought him and I were made for each other.

Happy: First impressions aren't always right, you know.

You: Well even so, I'm gutted by it all at the moment. I really liked him. We'd been together six months. I honestly thought he was the one, you know.

Happy: Hey, come on, don't get down about it. It obviously wasn't meant to be. You'll have forgotten about him in a couple of months.

You: I'm not so sure, I …

Happy: Come on, cheer up. You know what my mum always says, 'There's plenty more fish in the sea.'

You: But I don't want a fish … I want a man

The impact of a happy

Sometimes people can make mountains out of molehills. When this occurs, a 'happy' can bring a sense of perspective with their approach. Listening to them can help us appreciate that things are not as bad as they first might seem.

But their approach can also be equally unhelpful. By constantly trying to look on the bright side or 'sweep things under the carpet' with false reassurances, they can send the message 'negative feelings are not valid'. People can be made to feel guilty when they want to express their disappointment or frustration. Rather than listening to you and making you feel your emotions are appropriate, happies are in the habit of vacuuming up any hint of negativity. Issues are not explored and people are not given an opportunity to express their feelings.

Perhaps most worryingly, a happy can trivialise important issues. Their approach to 'Moving On' is to achieve happy feelings in the shortest possible time. Rather than deal with reality and work towards a solution – which may take time – they hope to bypass genuine emotions and achieve arrival in the promised land of sugar-coated happiness as quickly as possible.

I once came across the following quote from an unknown writer – I sense most happies would like this as a sign on their wall.

'A positive attitude may not solve all your problems, but it will annoy enough people to make it worth the effort.'

A happy can make a mountain into a molehill.

SUMO
wisdom

The happy's side of the beachball

Life is too short to be miserable. I believe it's far better to focus on what's going well. I like to **S**hut **U**p on the negative and quickly **M**ove **O**n to the positive or else we both might drown in a sea of despondency and despair.

People like to be cheered up and that's what I do. When people are feeling down, my philosophy is, 'There's no use crying over spilt milk.' I see it as my job to pick them up, to remind them of the positives and to make them feel better. Most people appreciate that, don't they?

I'm happy when others are happy. I hate it when others are despondent or disappointed. Sometimes I'm not sure what to say. You see I don't like silence, so I usually find something to be positive about.

I guess what I'm also saying is I feel uncomfortable when people are expressing negative emotions.

I feel that by telling me their problems, people are somehow expecting me to sort them out, it's just that I don't always know how to. But I am good at trying to keep things in perspective, which I hope brings comfort and makes people feel better. That's what I try to do. You can't blame me for that, can you?

Can it ever be helpful to be a happy?

Absolutely. We've already outlined many reasons – when a trivial issue is being blown out of perspective then a happy approach could be perfect. Equally, when someone has been hanging out with the hippos for too long and wallowing to excess, then it may just be time to turn to a happy to help them move on.

How to ~~handle~~ not strangle a happy

Let's be very clear. Some of the attitudes and behaviours demonstrated by a happy are to be encouraged and valued.

Looking on the bright side of life can be very helpful. Being positive is to be encouraged. But happies need to realise their outlook to life needs also to be accompanied by some balance, skill and sensitivity.

Let happies know that you appreciate their perspective on life and that you understand their motives are driven by a desire to be helpful. But express your expectations – let the happy know it's not cheering up you need at the moment, but just someone who will listen to you.

If a happy says …	You might want to say …
Come on, look on the bright side.	I appreciate you're trying to be really helpful and supportive, but I'm not ready to look on the bright side yet. It would really help me if you just let me talk things through.
I'm sure everything will be alright.	I value the fact that you're remaining optimistic, but I think we do need to explore some practical ways to move forward.
Well, they had a good innings.	Yes they did, but that doesn't make things any less painful at the moment.
You'll be fine.	I'm sure I will eventually but you just need to know I'm finding things difficult at the moment.

How to handle the happy in yourself

1   **Shut Up** believing everyone needs cheering up.

    Move On to recognising Hippo Time is necessary for people on occasions.

2   **Shut Up** thinking you have to think of something positive to say.

    Move On to just being there for people

3   **Shut Up** being insensitive with your remarks ('Cheer up, they had a good innings').

    Move On to being more sensitive and compassionate in your response.

4   **Shut Up** offering glib reassurances.

    Move On to exploring and offering practical solutions.

SUMO pit stop

- Who are the happies in your life?

- Do you need to be more honest about what you require from them sometimes?

- Do you tend to be a happy?

- What would be a more helpful way of helping someone?

Positivity Pays

We've already looked at the importance of our attitude when it comes to developing better relationships with others. Now in this insight, I'd like to explore more specifically how choosing a positive focus and creating positive impressions can reduce conflict and enhance relationships.

I'm often referred to as a motivational speaker. So when someone asks me how I am, they're not expecting the typical British reply 'not bad'. I don't usually disappoint, although I rarely go as far as the American motivational speaker Zig Ziglar, whose usual reply to that question is 'I'm outstanding, but I'll get better.' Mancunian motivational speakers tend to be a little more understated.

So why am I telling you this? Well, despite generally being a positive person, I still find it incredibly easy to slip into a negative outlook on life – particularly in terms of what I think of other people. There can be times when I find myself being sucked into the trap of continual fault finding. Ask me what I think of someone and I'll give you an overview of a person's qualities – but I don't leave it at that. I still feel the need to highlight a person's shortcomings. So I might say 'Tony is a great guy, but probably not the world's greatest time keeper.' It might be true. But is it necessary for me to say it at this point? Don't get me wrong, I'm very aware that it's not always helpful or appropriate to ignore people's negative behaviours. But neither do I believe we should view a person through the lens of a magnifying glass and focus purely on their negative characteristics. This simply gives us a distorted and unbalanced perspective of people.

SUMO wisdom

Every time you give an opinion, you reveal something about yourself.

SUMO pit stop

If the meaning of this piece of SUMO wisdom isn't immediately obvious, think about it a bit more.

Here's a great piece of advice. Before we embark upon a fault-finding mission about another person, it would be worth heeding the words of the Jewish Carpenter we mentioned earlier in the book. His advice was this:

> *Before you remove the speck from another person's eye, remove the plank from your own.*

Ouch. Wise words, don't you think?

So why do we focus on the negative?

There are many reasons for this – here are four:

- **A question of trust.** Maybe we've been hurt by people in the past. Our trusting nature backfired and we now tend to be much more cautious and suspicious of others. Focusing on the negative aspects of people can be our way of not getting close to someone. Our negativity becomes a self-defence mechanism designed to protect ourselves from being hurt. After all, if I see the negative in you, it gives me a reason not to trust you.

- **We feel better about ourselves.** When we compare ourselves favourably with others by seeing the negative aspects in their character, we in turn can feel more positive about ourselves.

- **We like to spread a little criticism.** Some people spend so much time being self-critical, that this way of thinking impacts how they also see others. Why confine our criticism to ourselves when we can spread it around?

- **We play judge and jury.** Some people believe there is only one way of viewing the world – and that's their way. Anyone who acts and thinks differently is clearly wrong. These people have no concept of the SUMO principle 'Remember the beachball' and whilst I'm not suggesting we abandon all our beliefs and values in order to build better relationships, I am suggesting we adopt a more flexible perspective in how we see others.

So how can we develop positivity to help our relationships? Here are two ideas:

Seek and you shall find

We've talked previously about your RAS, your Reticular Activating System. It helps filter information so that you only notice things that are relevant, important, of interest, or highly unusual. Hence, if you're thinking of buying another car, you suddenly see that particular car everywhere. (When this happened to me, I never realised how many Ladas there were in the UK.) Perhaps of equal significance is that your RAS filters *out* information that is not considered relevant or important.

So the types of car I wasn't considering buying were completely ignored. I didn't notice them.

In terms of relationships, this has important consequences. If someone has created a negative first impression, it can be difficult to see beyond this initial impact. We notice other behaviour to support and reinforce our view and can completely ignore any positive traits they may possess. If we're not prepared to give someone a second chance, then it's very difficult to notice positive behaviour. So what do you do? Re-tune your RAS. I am not suggesting we ignore the negative, simply that we develop a more balanced perspective. Ask yourself questions such as:

• What are some of this person's positive traits?

• How could I see their behaviour in a more positive way?

• What are four things I like about this person? (That might be a stretch, but in most cases should be possible ... go on, give it a try.)

I appreciate there's going to be times when you don't want to reflect on such questions. The behaviour of the other person may be completely unacceptable. But there will be occasions when such questions will help us to develop a more balanced perspective and may save the relationship.

SUMO wisdom

What you focus on magnifies.

SUMO pit stop

Be honest. Are you struggling with your attitude towards someone at present? Are you prepared to think about some of these questions? If not, fine. It's your choice. But if you do, it might influence how you interact with them next time and therefore the way the relationship plays out over the long term.

The work stuff

I'd been running a workshop on how to coach and counsel challenging employees. I stressed it was important to end your meeting on a positive note. 'What if you can't think of anything positive to say?' asked one of the group. 'Tell them they breathe well and you like the way they walk', piped up a colleague.

Create positive impressions

I was temped not to use the phrase, 'You never get a second chance to make a first impression', as it's become such a cliché. I hate clichés (although I'd be over the moon if you'd not come across the quote before). However, cliché or not, it happens to be true. As I'm meeting new people every day, I'm acutely aware of the need to create positive first impressions. As human beings, we're all quick to judge others. A way of coping with the deluge of information that is constantly being fired at the brain is to pigeon-hole people. Once I've categorised you, it makes life easier for me. As we mentioned before, when you meet someone for the first time, your appearance, height, weight, strength of handshake and whether or not you make any eye contact or smile, all create an impression – and that's before you start talking. The initial impression you make can form the foundation for the rest of your relationship.

First impressions aren't always right – but they are powerful.

SUMO wisdom

The work stuff

I was running a workshop on 'influencing skills'. I arrived early in order to set up the room. Marion, a delegate, also arrived early. We briefly exchanged greetings and she sat down to read her paper. Having now done all I needed to do in terms of preparation, I became very aware of the silence in the room. It was deafening. I decided to engage Marion in some further small talk. I noticed she was studying the house section of her paper.

'Thinking of moving house?' I enquired.

'Is that any of your bloody business?' replied Marion.

Call me intuitive, but I sensed she wasn't comfortable with small talk. Marion was there to learn how to influence people. She might have been a Cambridge graduate, but when it came to her social and interpersonal skills, her education was sorely lacking. She made a first impression I'll never forget.

The personal stuff

Personally I blame the cats. Ever since we've had them, we've had to programme our house alarm differently because of where they hang out in the house. Recently, Helen and I failed to programme the alarm correctly and as we set off to see friends, we were blissfully unaware that our neighbours were about to receive a loud awakening. This happened twice in the space of seven days. We knew they'd been forgiving the first time, but realised they'd be less so the second. Helen and I applied 'Positivity Pays'. On our return we immediately went out and bought some flowers and then went round to each neighbour to apologise in person. We didn't wait for their rebuke, we were pro-active. At the heart of being positive is a desire to be a bridge builder and to work at creating an impression and an environment whereby relationships can flourish. Our neighbours were both surprised but also appeased by our approach – we're still on speaking terms and our relationships remain intact.

Creating a positive impact and being pro-active can help diffuse a potentially difficult situation. It can also help create an environment where relationships can grow. The first few minutes of any encounter can set the tone for the rest of the interaction. That's why Positivity Pays.

The personal stuff

My friend and fellow business speaker, Steve McDermott, talks about the 'four-minute rule'.

Steve works away a great deal. So when he returns home he just often wants some peace and quiet. Now, for Steve to achieve this state of nirvana would probably mean him ignoring his wife and three children and forming a close relationship with the TV remote control and a can of beer.

He's realised from past experience that such behaviour is rarely greeted with any enthusiasm from his family.

Here's what he decided to do.

As he gets close to home, he thinks, 'How would a really great husband and father act in the first four minutes of returning home?' Then that's how he aims to behave for the first few minutes. (I'm not suggesting he carries a stopwatch with him though.) Steve finds if the first few minutes with his family are fairly positive and upbeat, it then usually sets the tone for the rest of the evening.

When I first heard Steve's four-minute rule, I felt like crawling into a corner. The reason? My initial greeting when I arrived home was to exclaim, 'Who's left all these shoes in the porch and will you hang up your coats for goodness sake.' Helen, with a dash of sarcasm, would reply 'Hi love. You obviously had a good journey home.'

However, I have to say that Matt and Ruth don't always greet me in quite the way I'd wish. If it's a choice between engaging in some brief small talk with their father or watching their favourite television programme, I rarely get a look in. (So kids, if you're reading this, remember what to do when the old man gets back from work next time.)

SUMO pit stop

- What are your thoughts on the four-minute rule? What usually happens when you arrive home from work or from an outing?

- Where does positivity apply in your workplace?

Right, now make sure you're sitting down for the next question – it's potentially very challenging:

- If your partner was to meet you today for the very first time, would they want to meet you again?

Positive impressions at work

A great way to create a positive impression at work is in relation to how you conduct meetings. Want to alienate and demotivate people and create an environment where people want to strangle each other? Then run unstructured, unfocused meetings that rarely start on time. No? So do the opposite, be on time and be prepared. Not exactly a revolutionary idea – but not one that's occurred to everyone.

> **SUMO wisdom**
>
> Being late occasionally is understandable. To do so regularly shows a complete lack of respect for other people.

I would like to emphasise that the above SUMO wisdom is written particularly from a British perspective. The key, I would suggest, is that when working in a particular culture, you respect the cultural norms and values. In Britain, that means being on time whenever possible.

Your SUMO takeaway

Positivity does pay. It is not a magic wand or some slick sales trick designed to flatter people. Neither is it intended to deny the existence of negative behaviour in others. But it is an attitude of mind that encourages us to be more conscious of the impression we're making – particularly on those we see most often.

It's also a challenge not to embark on a daily fault-finding mission, but to look for the positives in people. That might be harder to do with some people than others, but it could help you develop a more rounded and less distorted picture of people. At the very least, it might make your next interaction a less negative one. (You may even quit fantasising about strangling them.) You will also find that people who think positively tend to feel more positive about themselves, life and relationships … something which our next SUMO character would benefit from knowing.

My SUMO takeaway from 'Positivity Pays' is …

The Whinger

Why you may want to strangle a whinger

Whingers are a member of the BMW family – Bitching, Moaning Whingers. If they won the lottery, they'd probably say, 'Just my luck it wasn't a rollover week.' Focusing on the positive is an anathema to them. Life for a whinger seems to be a journey to be endured rather than enjoyed and many of the great joys of life just seem to pass them by.

They're only happy when they're miserable.

Their joy is having something to moan about.

They embrace misery like a long-lost friend, they wear doom and gloom like a favourite old coat. Whingers have lots to say about what's wrong with the world and why 'the management', 'the government', etc. haven't got a clue. They focus on problems. Solutions are not their territory – someone else should be coming up with those. Their mission is to remind people that there's plenty of negative things to be unhappy about.

A whinger in conversation in the workplace

You: What did you think of the meeting?

Whinger: Hopeless. For a start, who chose that hotel? The coffee was cold and they'd run out of biscuits when I arrived.

You: You were twenty minutes late.

Whinger: Yeah and you know why that was? Flipping traffic. Whoever designed that new one-way system needs shooting. My granny could have done a better job and she was blind from the age of seven.

You: Well others managed to get there on time.

Whinger: Yeah, but when I arrived there were no parking spaces. Why did we choose a hotel that's got a leisure centre? The car park was full of poncy women going to the gym. Haven't they got better things to do with their time?

You: OK and what about the meeting? I want to know how you feel about the proposed changes, particularly the re-branding of your department.

Whinger: How much did we pay some stupid consultant to come up with the title 'Service Excellence Centre'?

You: So what would you have called it?

Whinger: Well what's wrong with its current name, 'The Complaints Department'? I don't see anything wrong with that.

You: No, I sensed you wouldn't. And it's a pity Sue Mathers is leaving. I thought the new name for her role was great.

Whinger: What was that then?

You: Head of Motivation.

Whinger: Em … I might apply for that. I could do with a change.

A whinger in conversation outside the workplace

Whinger: I hate trains. They're never on time. And they're always overcrowded.

You: It's not due for another ten minutes. You never know, you might be in luck today.

Whinger: Luck? Don't talk to me about luck. I'm one of the unluckiest people I know. If Madonna had given birth to triplets, I'd have been the one she'd bottle fed. I've got to be the unluckiest person I know. Do you know I've never won a thing in my life. Not a single thing. Not even a tenner on the lottery.

You: Well maybe your luck will change. Anyway, I'm looking forward to a nice, relaxing journey. I've upgraded us to first class, so it should be a real treat.

Whinger: First class? How much did that cost?

You: Relax, it's my treat.

Whinger: What's wrong with standard class like everyone else?

You: I just thought we deserved a treat. And they serve breakfast.

Whinger: I bet they don't do porridge. Anyway, I've eaten already.

You: Well just chill out and read the paper.

Whinger: The paper? Why would I want to read the paper? It's full of doom and gloom.

You: Precisely.

The impact of a whinger

A whinger's constant mantra of moaning and their pessimistic outlook can have a demoralising effect on others. They give their opinion even when it's not asked for. Their presence at work, at home, or in a social gathering can be like a dull toothache. It's not painful enough to need removing, but it eats away at your enjoyment. Whingers either attract other whingers (in which case they set up a BMW Club) or they find they have to get used to their own company as people avoid them (thus giving them another opportunity to moan about how unfriendly people are). Enthusiasm, creativity and energy all need to take evasive action when they come under fire from a whinger's comments. Their constant bombardment of negativity can wear down the most positive of people. And perhaps of most concern, a whinger as a parent or spouse can drain the self-belief and confidence of their children and partner.

In recent years, we've become aware of the potential threat of passive smoking, i.e. you personally don't have to be smoking to suffer from its effects, you just need to be in the company of people that do. The same goes for whinging. If you spend enough time with whingers, their comments have the potential to pollute your mind and change your outlook.

Government warning — being around whingers can seriously damage your health.

SUMO
wisdom

The whinger's side of the beachball

The world is not pink and fluffy. It's hard, it's tough, it's full of disappointments. People let you down as I know from personal experience. As for Management, they come up with a great idea one month, and before you know it, they've changed their mind and are doing something different the next. We go through new initiatives in the same way people try out different-flavoured ice creams.

Be honest – hasn't the same thing happened where you work?

Everywhere I go, people, organisations, governments, all have one thing in common … they over-promise and under-deliver. Haven't you found that?

Some people call me a pessimist or claim I'm just cynical. I'm neither.

I'm a realist. And the reality is, life is not always what it's cracked up to be.

I don't know about you, but I can't stand those positive motivational type of people. They must be living on another planet. They ought to open their eyes more and see things for what they really are. It's alright for them coming out with their crass and banal superficial statements … 'Let's be positive' or 'Problems are what you see when you take your eye off the goal'. Give me a break. I've tried being positive – it doesn't work. It only sets you up for more disappointment; wouldn't you agree?

In many respects my view of life is, 'expect the worst and you won't be disappointed.' As mottos go, I'm happy with that. Can you understand where I'm coming from?

The work stuff

I used to work with a whinger called Bill. He seemed to thrive on being miserable. He was also an expert in anticipating things going wrong.

He had two favourite sayings, 'It'll never work', and 'The week's dragging'. (The later was invariably said about mid-morning on a Monday.)

Deep down, I think he quite liked this whinging role. It gave him an identity. I even found his comments amusing at times. But if I'd had a bad day, I avoided Bill. I could cope with his negativity when I was feeling positive. In fact, we'd end up playing 'attitude tennis' together. He'd serve me a negative comment and I'd return it back to him with a heavy dose of top-spin positivity.

But when I was down emotionally, I found his negative 'serves' harder to return.

Can it ever be helpful to be a whinger?

I've really thought about this – and here's my conclusion. No.

How to handle not strangle a whinger

- Recognise that some people are born with a propensity to be more pessimistic or melancholic in outlook. Maybe it's in their genes, so be a little more tolerant.

- Don't dismiss their moaning out of hand entirely. Beneath their whinging, there may be some very genuine and valid concerns. Your goal should be to go beyond the 'noise' of their whinging and find out what the real issues are.

- Remember a whinger's comments may be born out of some very real disappointment that now manifests itself in disillusionment with people and with life in general. Understand how past hurts may be influencing their current outlook.

- Communicate your side of the beachball. Spell out the impact and consequences of their moaning on the people around them. Help them to realise that although they may mean no harm, their comments could be undermining the morale and self belief of others.

- Help them to moan in a more constructive way.

It's OK for them to express their unhappiness or dissatisfaction with something, but they must be prepared to explain why they are unhappy and provide some helpful ways to improve the situation. You could adapt SUMO question number four 'How can you or I influence or improve the situation?' You are not necessarily trying to silence the whinger (although there will be times when that is totally appropriate), but to help them realise that it's in everyone's interest to focus on moving on.

So for example, if the train is 'always late', what could they be doing in the meantime?

Whingers often wear victim T-shirts. They don't look for solutions, they look to see who's to blame. Help them to understand that how they see a problem and personally respond to a situation can ultimately affect the outcome. (It might be worth them reading the chapter E + R = O.)

- Welcome their negativity on occasions. Sometimes teams or committees can get carried along under a tidal wave of optimism. A reality check would be helpful. A different perspective may be required. An optimist's blind spot may need to be pointed out.

- However, rather than saying, 'Let's hear the whinger's view on this', we might want to 'big up' their input, perhaps by saying, 'OK, we might need a reality check here. Can I ask ... for their perspective?' You might even give them the title 'Reality Checker', but make sure they have clear guidelines on how to express their comments in a more positive and constructive way.

- Recognise that we all need a moan sometimes. Let's just make sure it's an occasional part of our experience and not the main reason for our existence.

If a whinger says ...	You may want to say ...
I've never enjoyed working here.	That's sad. What makes you feel that way?
It'll never work.	Why do you say that? What do you think would work?
They haven't a clue what they're doing.	So if you were in their position what could you do?
Expect the worst, that's my motto.	Has there ever been a time when things did work out better than you expected?

How to handle the whinger in yourself

1 **Shut Up** focusing on the negatives.

   Move On to finding the positives in a situation.

2   **Shut Up** whinging and complaining.

    Move On to communicating your concerns in an asser-
    tive and constructive manner.

3   **Shut Up** seeing yourself as a victim.

    Move On to seeing yourself as a survivor and ultimately
    a thriver.

4   **Shut Up** demotivating others.

    Move On to being more aware of your impact on people
    around you.

SUMO pit stop

Is there enough evidence to convict you of being a
whinger? If so, what factors have influenced this
outlook on life?

Have you thought about the impact you may be having on others?

If you deal regularly with a whinger, which strategy
or insight on how to handle not strangle them will be of most
help to you at the moment?

Confront With Care

It has to be one of the most challenging aspects of any relationship – having to confront a person about a particular issue. Our approach may vary depending on the context, but it's rarely a road easily travelled. Handled badly, it's got the potential to cause lasting long-term damage.

When it comes to drawing upon wisdom and insight as to how to handle such challenging situations, let's first of all explore a well known proverb.

Let sleeping dogs lie

For some people, the very thought of confronting someone provokes a release of stress hormones similar to those experienced by our prehistoric ancestors when they stumble across a sabre tooth tiger whilst out doing their weekly shopping.

I meet very few people who actually relish the thought of confronting others. Tact, skill and diplomacy are all required, but when was the last time we got some advice on how to do it effectively? It's much easier and far less hassle to simply do nothing.

On occasions I genuinely believe this might be the best approach. In order to maintain the peace, we may decide for the good of our long term relationship, not to aggravate the situation.

It may be you decide to lose the battle (by not addressing an issue) in order to achieve some form of longer-lasting peace.

This approach can be most effective when our existing relationship with someone is already fragile, or when on reflection, you realise that the issue you are thinking of tackling is not really that important. Perhaps the SUMO question 'Where is this issue on a scale of 1–10? (where 10 = death)' or asking yourself, 'How important will this be in six months' time?' can bring a sense of perspective to the situation.

But is this always the best approach? It would be great if it was. But it's not. Choosing not to confront an issue can cause the following:

- **Avoidance can be seen as a sign of weakness** on your part that some people are happy to exploit further. (Children are skilled masters at pushing the boundaries with parents or carers when they know they are too weak or inconsistent to impose some form of discipline.) When we become known as a soft touch, our credibility rating can plummet to zero which can lead to a complete loss of respect.

- **Avoidance can be viewed as acceptance.** Not tackling an issue can send the signal that you see nothing wrong with a person's current behaviour. Silence can be misinterpreted as acceptance.

- **Avoidance can lead to escalation.** Problems that initially appeared minor can, if not 'nipped in the bud', escalate and spread. One person's behaviour can become the accepted norm. If they can get away with it, why shouldn't I?

Additionally:

- Human nature dictates that people feel almost obliged to see just how much they can get away with before you finally say something.

SUMO wisdom

Peace in the short term may still be a recipe for war in the long term.

The work stuff

Although most people are uncomfortable with confrontation, it's not always the case. I was once running a workshop for managers and as part of the introductions, asked what were some of the things they enjoyed about work. One woman answered, 'Disciplining people.'

She was an interesting character and one to avoid on a dark night.

When I started life as a manager, I guess one thing I was particularly keen to achieve was popularity. I wanted to be liked. So when it came to confronting a particular secretary about her standard of work, I ended up apologising for having to discuss the issue. Eventually I received some much-needed advice from an experienced manager: 'Paul, if you wanted to be popular, you should have become a Red Coat at Butlins.'

The next piece of SUMO wisdom is, I believe, crucial especially to managers;

It's more important to be respected than to be liked.
To be liked is desirable,
to be respected is essential.

SUMO wisdom

SUMO pit stop

Several years ago I heard an American trainer called Harry Chambers use the following quotes:

'We receive the behaviour (or performance) we are willing to tolerate'; and

'My silence, denial or avoidance gives approval to the situation.'

Their relevance and importance still resonate with me today.

Reflect on the above quotes:

- Is there a situation with someone that you should not be tolerating?

- What are the consequences of being silent, denying or avoiding the problem?

- Is it better to let sleeping dogs lie on this occasion?

Confronting with care

When you've decided you need to tackle an issue with someone, we need guidance on how best to go about it. Let's focus on six really important points to help the process.

1 Avoid striking whilst the iron is hot.

At times, it's important to take action, but remember:

> **SUMO wisdom**
>
> Sometimes, when you strike whilst the iron is hot, people get burnt.

When you talk to a colleague, customer, member of staff, your partner or children, avoid, whenever you can, speaking out in the heat of the moment. We're unlikely to be in a calm or composed mood and our comments are likely to generate more heat than light. Even a ten-second break can help you in such situations.

Easy to do? Not in my experience.

But just because it's not easy doesn't mean it's not an approach to strive for. In a work situation, we often seem more prepared to consider our response, but our self-control can be far less resolute in our personal lives.

The personal stuff

A few days ago, I was sitting in our conservatory. (If you read my first SUMO book, you'll be glad to hear the roof is fixed.) Matthew, Ruth and their cousin Alex were sitting around the kitchen table. All was calm. Suddenly there was a commotion as the kids began to play-fight. I had my back to the whole proceedings from where I was sitting, but with the door slightly ajar, I could hear every verbal exchange – this was interesting, as the kids, it seemed, were unaware of my presence in the next room.

Matthew and Ruth have been known to fall out on occasions. When I say 'on occasions', there was a week last year when this didn't happen – Matthew was away on a school trip to France.

This occasion, however, it seemed their play-fighting had quickly overstepped the mark. Ruth was hurt – certainly judging by the crying I could hear. Matthew was less than concerned. As Ruth sobbed, she was met by a far from compassionate response: 'Stop crying you wuss', Matthew said in a mocking tone.

There have been occasions in the past when Ruth has been easily upset. Her reactions have been akin to that of a footballer who's received the slightest nudge from an opposing player – completely disproportionate to the offence committed. But not on this occasion. From what I could hear, Matthew's behaviour towards his sister was totally out of order.

Moments earlier, I'd been calmly relaxing, reading a book about Bradford City's greatest achievements (I had ten minutes to kill and I'm a slow reader). Now I was ready to read the riot act to Matthew. As I heard the word 'wuss' fired at Ruth once again I decided to pounce. In the past I would have taken action first and asked questions later. Now, despite my feelings of rapidly increasing anger I took a moment to compose myself.

Matthew could have no defence. The evidence was overwhelming and I had heard it all. I rose from my seat and turned to face them. Mr Motivational Speaker (as the kids occasionally call me) was about to do his stuff.

But what greeted my eyes surprised me. Matt, Ruth and Alex all stood laughing at me. It had been a wind up. They'd known all along that I was in the conservatory.

Their acting skills were to be applauded

I felt relief that Matthew had not completely destroyed the view I had of him and relief also that I had not over-reacted and made myself look a complete fool. It was amusing. But it also made me aware how easy it can be to strike whilst the iron is hot – when you don't have all the facts.

SUMO pit stop

- What presses your hot buttons?

- Do you need to spend less time with a hot iron in your hand?

- What steps can you take to help you respond more rationally when necessary?

2 Focus on the facts.

Emotions are incredibly powerful in how they govern and influence our behaviour. Feelings can fluctuate wildly and distort our view of reality. They can cause us to use emotive and unhelpful language when engaging with others. Describing someone as 'lazy' may *feel* like an accurate description, but it immediately puts the other person on the defensive. Such a statement invites no opportunity for discussion or dialogue. Progress is minimal.

So focus on the facts as they appear to you. To do so, you have to step beyond your emotions (valid though they may be), and concentrate on specific behaviour. What behaviour are you seeing or not seeing that indicates this person is not helping or performing in a way that you believe is appropriate?

To answer such a question, you have to engage rational brain. You're forced to calm down – perhaps not to a state of being completely chilled, but certainly less heated than you might have been.

> *If you're not ready to focus on the facts, you're not ready to confront the other person.*

SUMO wisdom

3 Listen Loud to their side of the beachball.

We've spent two chapters already exploring these ideas. Remember, confrontation isn't simply about you doing the talking. Until you listen and find out how things look from their perspective, you won't have all the facts. You may discover something that completely alters your perspective – alternatively, you may not. Either way, this approach helps clarify your understanding of the situation.

4 Spell out the consequences and the impact.

It can be easy to highlight the behaviour you're not happy with, but without actually spelling out the consequences and impact of such actions.

For instance, some people might fail to see the big deal about being late if they're not aware of how it might affect other members of the team, or have not considered the impression it creates with customers or clients.

Likewise, some people seem happy to live in the midst of chaos and clutter and are totally oblivious as to how this affects those around them. It's time to communicate your side of the beachball and focus on the facts in terms of how this person's behaviour is affecting you and those around them.

5 Seek or state solutions.

Confrontation should have a purpose. It's not simply a time for letting off steam, although that can be helpful if done in a way that doesn't harm the other person. Neither is it an opportunity to pour blame and bile upon the head of the other person – however tempting that might be. The intention behind confrontation is to see an improvement in a situation that ideally is acceptable and agreeable to both sides. Remember:

SUMO wisdom

Shut Up trying to fix the blame.
Move On to fixing the problem.

Before confronting an individual, consider the following questions:

- Why do I feel the need to do this?

- What are the consequences if I avoid tackling the issue?

- Can I live with the consequences if I don't tackle the issue?

- Am I clear on the facts?

- Am I prepared to listen to their side of the beachball?

- What solution would be acceptable to me?

- Is that a fair solution for both parties?

Our desire to rush in to resolve an issue can blind us to the fact that we haven't considered what we would see as an acceptable solution. As Stephen Covey says:

SUMO wisdom

Begin with the end in mind.

How can you come to a solution that is acceptable to both parties? Firstly you need to agree there is a problem that needs resolving. Then having followed the ideas previously mentioned, ask the other person a question such as:

- 'So if you were me what would you do?'

- 'How do you think we could improve things?'

- 'I'd be interested in some of your ideas on how we can resolve this.'

- 'What do you suggest is the first thing we need to do?' or

- 'From your perspective, what do you think is the most important action we can take to improve the situation?'

Now here's a question to ask yourself. Whose ideas are we most enthusiastic about? Answer? Usually our own.

So when we seek solutions from the other person, we're more likely to get their co-operation. We're also maintaining their self respect by giving them an opportunity to be involved in improving the situation.

When you're involved in coming up with a solution, you're more committed to making it work.

SUMO
wisdom

But be careful. There is a danger in seeking solutions from others – they might not be acceptable to you. That's why it's helpful to ask a question such as, 'Let's explore some possible solutions', as you're implying there could be more than one.

On occasions, there may be no alternative, but to state the outcome you require. This could be due to the needs of the business; or it's a matter of health and safety; or simply because the other person lacks the emotional maturity, experience or knowledge to be able to propose an acceptable solution.

6 End on a positive note.

Confrontation is rarely easy. And even if one party recognises they may be in the wrong and a solution is agreed upon, it can still feel uncomfortable at the end of the conversation. That's why, whenever possible, practical and appropriate, it's helpful to end on a positive note.

For example, a manager finishing a meeting about a member of staff's performance might say, 'I appreciate your time and I look forward to seeing things improve. Our review meeting is in two weeks, but you know where I am if you need me.'

If you've had to confront a child about their behaviour it's important you follow up with reassurance. Giving them a hug or stating your love for them are hugely important in helping them to understand that after confrontation comes reconciliation.

The work stuff

I'd like to say I'm a stranger to confrontation. I'm not.

Some time ago, I hired the services of a small PR company and dealt exclusively with the owner, Alan. Our initial meeting in London established his credibility. Although quick at times to draw the conversation back to himself, he also asked what I considered to be insightful questions and suggested some effective and achievable ways to help raise my profile and the SUMO brand.

He was slow to send through his proposal to me but I put this down to his busyness, rather than sloppiness on his part. We agreed I would use his services for an initial three month period and he explained that much of the fruit of the campaign would not be seen until the third month.

Over the next month I heard very little from Alan, but recognised that in the early stages of the campaign a lot of behind the scenes work was being done. I paid his invoice promptly.

In the second month, we did have a ten-minute conversation about the progress of his work and I blocked out three days in my diary for the following month in order that media interviews could be arranged. The second invoice was paid.

Alan's services did not come cheaply.

Then, three days before I was due to travel to London, the significant PR breakthrough I'd hoped for came. One of the major TV stations wanted me to appear as a guest on a breakfast programme called LK Today. I would be the guest of Lorraine Kelly on her Friday morning show. I was delighted. With a further eight interviews lined up, including one with a leading national papers, I was beginning to feel justified in the decision I'd made to hire Alan.

Two weeks later I was regretting I'd ever heard of the guy's name. Not a single one of the media interviews in London took place. The excuses from Alan were endless. Double bookings. Journalists falling sick just minutes before their meeting me. One journalist even went on maternity leave unexpectedly early. To see two or three interviews fall through at the last minute was believable – but all eight?

During my pointless tour of London, with my frustration growing rapidly by the minute, I decided to stop speaking to Alan by phone. Emotionally I didn't feel in the best place to carry out a constructive conversation with him. I decided to text him instead. This required more time and effort on my part, but it also helped me to consider what I was saying to him. My London fiasco came to an end.

Alan assured me that he would redeem my PR campaign and even delayed sending me his next invoice. Big deal. I was not appeased, but at least I had a prime-time television appearance to look forward to. Or did I? I couldn't prove it conclusively, but I was convinced that my doomed trip to London owed more to lies and deception than bad luck. Helen and I decided to turn detective. We contacted the

TV station. Their response? They'd never heard of me or my SUMO book and the Lorraine Kelly show isn't even on a Friday.

My initial reaction was not one of shock – I'd seen it coming – but of immense disappointment. What drove Alan to lie so blatantly and profusely? Again I decided that a phone call was not the appropriate method of communication at this stage and chose to email him.

Before I could compose my email, he emailed me. Alan explained that after a lengthy phone call with the producer on the Lorraine Kelly Show, my interview was to be re-scheduled, however, the good news was that the King and Queen of daytime British television, 'Richard and Judy', wanted me as a guest on their show. I contacted the producers of the programme – they'd never heard of me.

On a scale of 1–10 (where ten equals death), this situation didn't even come close to a ten. But it was still an issue.

Before contacting Alan to surprise him with the news that I'd uncovered his intricate web of lies and deception, I thought about what I still wanted to achieve. That was simple. I wanted my money back. In all the ensuing communication we had, I kept focusing on my end goal. An apology was worthless. Promises to rectify the problem were meaningless. And reasons for why he behaved the way he did were of no interest. I wanted my money back. I kept my communication clear, concise and professional. I spelt out the consequences to him if I didn't receive my money back. (I assure you, the term 'contract killer' was never mentioned.)

The lies didn't stop, the frustration grew, but nine weeks later I received my money.

In the above example, I guess I aimed to do the following:

1   I took time out to cool down before I confronted Alan.

2   I focused on my end goal (getting my money back) and refused to deviate.

3 I kept perspective in terms of how important an issue it really was.

SUMO pit stop

If you'd been faced with the same situation, what, if anything would you have done differently?

SUMO takeaway

Confronting people is rarely easy. It takes tact, skill and diplomacy. It also helps to choose the right moment to confront. Is there a case for letting 'sleeping dogs lie' and not tackling an issue? Sometimes. But beware the consequences when you avoid taking action.

If you do take action, remember:

1 Avoid striking whilst the iron is hot.

2 Focus on the facts.

3 Listen Loud to their side of the beachball.

4 Spell out the consequences and the impact.

5 Seek or state solutions.

6 End on a positive note (when possible).

As we explore our final SUMO Character, they, like all the others, will need to be confronted with care.

My SUMO takeaway from 'Confront With Care' is ...

S.U.M.O. TAKEAWAY

The Swinger

Why you may want to strangle a swinger

Despite the title, the term 'swinger' has nothing to do with sexual preferences, or what people got up to if they were alive in the 1960s. A swinger, in this context, is someone who swings from one emotion to another, often in a short period of time, or swings from one great idea to another, but rarely sustains their enthusiasm for long.

Let me elaborate.

It's Tuesday and a 'swinger' has had a great idea on how to start a new business. They've run it past a guy they met in the pub last night and it's all systems go. This is the big one. It's a plan that cannot fail. They've thought everything through. Well kind of anyway. No matter what you seek to do to dampen their enthusiasm, the swinger remains convinced that, 'this is the big one'. All you can do is listen. It wouldn't be easy to speak – the swinger would have to pause briefly for you to do so. They don't. Four weeks later their idea is dead. It got nowhere. Not to worry, they've had another idea and this one will definitely work …

Life can be great for a swinger. At least it was this morning, but it's now the afternoon. That bright, breezy, happy-go-lucky person now looks like they've won the lottery, but lost their ticket. Now it's all doom and gloom. The future is not bright, in fact it's quite the opposite. Actually the way they're feeling at the moment, there might as well not be a future.

Meanwhile back in the office, the swinger greets new changes with enthusiasm. Not only that, but they're eager to volunteer to help push forward new proposals. It seems obvious that the new changes will succeed.

Problems? Pitfalls? Don't be negative.

It's hard to contain the swinger's enthusiasm. A month into the project and the swinger is encountering problems. The changes are taking longer to implement than anticipated.

Enthusiasm has been replaced with apathy. The swinger is de-motivated.

However, there's a new project about to start which sounds far more exciting and they're looking for a team member with just the set of skills the swinger possesses. It's time to have a word with their boss. They now realise their skills would be much better suited on this other project. Surprisingly, their request is accepted. Six weeks later however …

A swinger in conversation

Swinger: How's things?

You: Well as weeks go, it's been fairly routine. Nothing much to report. You know me. I just keep plodding along. What about you?

Swinger: I've had an incredible week. In fact, it's been life-changing.

You: Really? Why, what happened?

Swinger: Well I went along to that property seminar I mentioned. You know, the one about buying cheap property in Poland.

You: Oh yeah, I remember you said you were going. What was it like?

Swinger: Absolutely incredible. They reckon Poland is going to be the new Bulgaria.

You: Bulgaria?

Swinger: Yeah. Weren't you aware how much property is now worth in Bulgaria compared with three years ago? If you bought property back then, you'd be able to sell it for thirty times what you paid for it

You: Incredible. How do you know?

Swinger: The guy running the seminar told us. He's a multi-millionaire property tycoon, so he should know what he's talking about. I tell you, this time next year, I'll be rich.

You: But you mentioned Poland, not Bulgaria.

Swinger: Yeah. Poland is going just like Bulgaria. If I can raise sufficient funds, I want to buy at least three properties out there and then flog them in three years.

You: So how much do you need to raise?

Swinger: Only £30,000. That should be easy to get from the bank.

You: You mean you've done a business plan already and done the sums on what you're likely to make?

Swinger: Well, not exactly.

You: Look, how do you know for sure that it's going to work?

Swinger: I just do. I can sense it in my bones.

You: But you said that last time when you started an emu farm.

Swinger: Oh that was different.

You: In what way?

Swinger: It just was. There wasn't a demand for the meat or the eggs.

You: But you were convinced you'd end up with farms all across Europe.

Swinger: Well these things happen.

You: But you're still in debt from borrowing money last time.

Swinger: Trust me. I just know this is going to work.

The impact of a swinger

It's not immediately obvious when you meet this kind of person, that they're actually a swinger. Perhaps not surprisingly, people don't wear a sign proclaiming, 'Hi, I'm a swinger'.

Initially you may be impressed with their enthusiasm and positivity. On the other hand, you may be concerned with how negative and down this person can be. (Most of the time they tend to oscillate between being a 'happy' and an 'awfuliser' and are rarely anything in between). Their mood swings can become tiring though. Once you realise their enthusiasm for a project will soon be replaced with something else, you fail to encourage their initiative.

You see them as being unreliable.

Empathy may also be lacking when you realise that, although today might seem like the end of the world to them, tomorrow could bring a whole set of different emotions.

The personal stuff

I took my daughter to her swimming lesson recently. (Yes I know: what an awesome father.) She didn't want to go. Helen and I had been away for the weekend and she had missed her mum. (Hey I can handle rejection.) Ruth was enjoying chilling out in the garden. She went to her lesson – under protest. Her distress in the car as we drove there was equivalent to her reaction when I offered to get her a season ticket to watch Bradford City.

I remained quiet. She fought back the tears. We arrived. I paid and she went in to get changed. Five minutes later, as I watched from the gallery, I saw her chatting with a friend before the lesson started. By the time she took to the pool, her whole demeanour had changed.

She's a good swimmer. Now I'm not a competitive father, but there was just a hint of pride as, along with other parents, I saw my special girl completely whoop the kids in her class in terms of speed and style. As she came out of the changing room, her face had the look of 'Didn't I do well Dad?' Her smile was on a par with when she heard me say, 'I was only joking about the Bradford City season ticket.'

I guess you could say my daughter had experienced a dramatic mood swing. She's eleven years old. Most children do. But the swinger behaves in a similar way. And sometimes it's tempting to say to them, 'Grow up.'

SUMO pit stop

- Do you swing much?

- Are your moods your master or are you mastering your moods?

The swinger's side of the beachball

I'm a swinger. As I see things, it's always important to listen to your intuition. Follow it at all costs. If an idea seems good, then go for it. Don't hold back.

Be a risk taker.

Being cautious is boring, don't you agree?

I thrive on excitement. Planning is a necessary evil. But you can get bogged down in plans, can't you? Action and enthusiasm are the keys to success.

Sometimes people play safe and look to do things the way they've always been done. Where's the excitement in that?

I'm an emotional person, I admit that. I wear my heart on my sleeve – you never have to guess how I'm feeling – you'll know. If you can't tell from my body language (and you should be able to), then I'll happily tell you. I don't believe in bottling up your feelings. It's unhealthy. Be true to yourself.

I believe passionately that you should follow your dreams. My motto is: *If at first you don't succeed – try something else.*

Can you see where I'm coming from?

Can it ever be helpful to be a swinger?

If you're looking for someone to generate new and fresh ideas mixed with bags of enthusiasm then turn to a swinger. If you're looking for someone to implement these ideas – turn to someone else.

How to handle not strangle a swinger

- Recognise there's a difference between occasional mood swings, which are normal and being a fully-blown swinger. It's also important to remember that some mood swings may be due to medical reasons and will need professional help.

- Remember that although they usually bounce back from a setback, the swinger may need reassurance that you're still there for them.

- Avoid immediately pouring cold water on their ideas. Some may have more potential than you first realise, they just may need a little more thinking through and planning.

- Encourage a swinger's progress. Your encouragement may help them develop their resilience and stickability.

- Challenge a swinger to see things through and not to give up too easily.

- Recognise the positive role they can have within a team, but the need to have others around who are stronger on strategy, discipline and detail.

- Do not have a swinger as a team leader. They might occasionally be the star player and be 'the man of the match' – but they rarely make great captains.

When a swinger says ...	You might want to say ...
I've had a brilliant idea about X and I'm convinced it will work.	That does sound interesting. Have you thought who might be able to help you with it?
I'm thinking of giving up on X. I don't feel very motivated at the moment.	What do you think is causing this lack of motivation? **OR** But how would you feel about yourself if you did decide to stick with X until it's completed?
I just think everything's going wrong for me at the moment	You sound down. How long have you felt this way? **OR** I appreciate you seem to be struggling at the moment. What can I do to help?
I think we should just go for it – what have we got to lose?	I certainly agree it might be worth taking action, but lets quickly review our options. **OR** I know this might sound negative, but lets reflect on what we might lose if we take that action.

Handling the swinger in yourself

1 **Shut Up** allowing yourself to be dominated by your feelings.

   Move On to mastering your emotions.

2   **Shut Up** the 'all or nothing' view on life.

   Move On to seeing things in perspective.

3   **Shut Up** taking action without thinking.

   Move On to planning then acting

3   **Shut Up** believing the world is about to end.

   Move On to asking, 'How important will this be in six months time?'

4   **Shut Up** thinking, 'Life must always be exciting.'

   Move On to recognising life is a mixture of the mundane, the ordinary and the exciting.

SUMO pit stop

- Do you encounter swingers in your life? How have you dealt with them previously?

- Which strategy or insight on how to handle them will most help your relationship?

SUMO Into Action

Well, as Frank Sinatra sang, 'And now the end is near and so I face the final curtain.' Reading a book can be a similar experience. You come to the end, put it back on the shelf and draw a curtain over your thoughts and ideas. You may feel inspired to change – but will you?

So here's my idea. Don't put the book on the shelf or lend it to a friend. My aim wasn't to provide you with a few pleasant thoughts and ideas that you can reflect on briefly and then forget about. My goal in writing was to provide you with a tool kit to help you build, maintain and restore your relationships. It's a job that lasts a lifetime, so some regular reflecting on how to achieve this will be required.

In order to help you do this, the idea I have is for you to use each day of the week as an opportunity to focus and reflect on one of the 'Seven SUMO Realities and Insights'. You may even want to create your own weekly plan that you keep somewhere visible to remind you of the actions you want to take.

And so it's over to you. No one can change your life but you. You're in the driving seat. Are you consciously engaged in the journey ahead or operating on cruise control? I reckon it's time for the excuses to stop, as it is for the habit of reading, learning and then failing to take action. So I hope the following helps the process.

Monday

SUMO action

Focus today on 'Arouse Your Attitude'. Remember how I'd become complacent by allowing myself to look down on

Mark? Think about your interactions with people today and work hard at levelling up that see-saw in terms of how you're viewing yourself and others.

Be aware

Reality Rules. You may make some mistakes and other people may respond to you in a way you'd not expected. Today you might see faults in others that you dislike within yourself. Be aware of that fact. And if you experience some conflict, remember it takes two to tango, so you may want to consider how you may be contributing to this conflict.

Today might be a good time to be a little more tolerant and forgiving of yourself and others. And whatever happens, think about these words from the American writer Ralph Waldo Emerson:

'Finish each day and be done with it. You have done what you could. Some blunders and absurdities have crept in; forget them as soon as you can. Tomorrow is a new day.'

Tuesday

SUMO action

Focus today on 'Humility Helps'. Think about the needs of at least one other person. Who could you ring or visit? Today could also be a good opportunity to ask someone for help. What's the worst they could say? If you experience some conflict, be prepared to reflect on your own behaviour. Do you need to apologise, say sorry and admit your mistakes to anyone? Finally, look for opportunities today to get some feedback from others – and whatever anyone says, look for the gold – the nuggets of insight that could prove invaluable.

Be aware

Whatever happens today, it's not simply the **E**vent that determines your **O**utcome, but how *you* **R**espond (**E + R = O**). Today, you might need to reflect on the SUMO question:

'Is my response appropriate and effective?'

Remember: you're not Pavlov's dog. You can choose to respond differently to events and the behaviour of others – if you want to.

Wednesday

SUMO action

Today, make a conscious effort to 'Listen Loud' to at least one other person. Will it be a colleague, customer, friend or family member? You decide. It's not always easy to do – but making the effort could help develop a more rewarding relationship.

Be aware

Remember other people's view of the beachball. Recognise that the people you're interacting with today may have a completely different perspective on a situation from you – and that perspective is valid for them. Recognise that differences can lead to misunderstandings, which is why it's crucial to Listen Loud. Reflect on Stephen Covey's advice:

'Seek first to understand.'

Thursday

SUMO action

Today, make a decision to 'Excel in Encouragement'. Think of someone who you want to specifically encourage. Maybe they've had a setback or disappointment, or maybe it's someone who you've perhaps been taking for granted and who needs to feel valued. Think about how you will encourage them. A card? A letter? A gift? A phone call? Give it some thought – it could make a huge difference.

Be aware

Stress makes you stupid. Be conscious that other people's behaviour may be symptomatic of their current levels of stress. Offer them support. And what about yourself? How are you managing your pressure? What do you need to be aware of in terms of managing your own stress levels?

And please, if you are feeling especially tired and emotional today, don't make any important decisions. Give yourself time to reflect and seek the support of others.

And remember:

How things look on the outside depends on what's going on in the inside.

Friday

SUMO action

Today, focus on 'Expressing Your Expectations'. Make sure you're expressing your needs rather than hoping others will guess what they are. Be realistic in your expectations, and if people aren't getting the message, it's up to you to clarify the picture. You may want to encourage someone to express their expectations of you in terms of your relationship today.

Be aware

Investment really does pay. Reflect on some of your key relationships. Is there a deficit in terms of the amount of time you're investing in each other? Are your expectations of this relationship realistic, given the current amount of time invested?

Remember, when you say you haven't got time, what you're really saying is:

'I've chosen to make something else more of a priority at the moment.'

Saturday

SUMO action

Your focus today is on 'Positivity Pays'. With the people you meet, look for some positives about their character and behaviour. It may not be easy, but look for some of their positive attributes anyway. If there was one thing you could admire or like about that person, what would it be?

And today, when you're meeting people, create a positive impression – even with the people you see on a daily basis. Think about how you will go about creating this positive impression.

Be aware

It's important to make sure you and those around you 'Get the VIP Treatment' regularly. It's crucial that you build in some rest, recovery and rejuvenation time for yourself. Plan, today, when this will happen. And when it comes to the demands that others place on you, reflect on the wise words of Andrew Matthews:

> *'We are happy in life, to the extent that we believe we have control over our circumstances – and taking control of our lives often means saying "no".'*

Sunday

SUMO action

Is there someone who you need to confront about an issue? If not, great. However, if you do think an issue needs resolving, do so with care. Remember, confronting an issue does not equate to being confrontational with a person. Make sure it's a battle worth fighting. If you need clarity on whether it is or not, ask yourself, 'Am I prepared to live with the consequences if I decide not to deal with the situation?' If you do confront, then focus, above all, on solutions and moving forward – refuse to play the blame game.

Be aware

Despite all our best intentions and use of various strategies, some people will not change. 'Light bulbs' come with the territory so don't allow their unwillingness to change to be seen as a failure on your part. Reflect on the fact that, with some people, it may just be a case of finding the right switch – with others, it's simply a case of recognising Reality Rules.

However, be encouraged. Probably only one or two per cent of people are genuine light bulbs. With the other ninety-eight per cent, you're now in a much better position to handle, not strangle, the people you live and work with.

Personal Postscript

I don't always find writing easy. It requires real discipline and I often wrestle for what seems like hours, trying to put down on paper what's inside my head.

I've written several books now, however writing this one has brought with it a set of new challenges I'd not previously encountered.

It's made me focus on my own relationships with the people I live and work with. And I've had to ask myself the hard question, 'Am I practising what I'm preaching?'

Then in the middle of writing this book, I had a major health scare.

During the summer I developed stomach trouble. Believing it to be nothing serious I went to the doctor expecting a reassuring word and the latest quick fix medicine to solve my problem. He gave me neither.

His opening question, 'Is there a history of bowel cancer in the family?' was not one I expected.

It knocked me off balance.

When you're off balance, you don't always respond effectively to life's challenges and there have been times in the last few months when I've been guilty of being far from effective in terms of my relationships with others. You see, I'm pretty good at helping others, but I've had to be very conscious of the SUMO Insight 'Humility Helps'.

I've needed to ask for the support and advice of a number of close friends – thankfully they've been happy to give it.

It's easy to think that people who write books about relationships have all the answers and none of the problems. I honestly wish that was true – but it isn't. If doctors can fall sick, why shouldn't someone who writes and speaks on relationships also have some challenges in this area? Like I stated in my introduction, what I write is born out of experience and not theory and I hope my insights are richer because of that.

In the midst of my challenges there's been some good news as well. Writing has also reinforced for me how helpful and relevant the ideas we've explored really are – they're truths that endure the test of time. They're not quick-fix solutions – repairing, restoring, renewing and even maintaining relationships takes time, effort and commitment.

Reflecting on this vast subject has also made me appreciate the importance of tolerance and compassion. Both are needed, but I find they're not always quite the priorities I should make them. I thought we became more tolerant with age – if that's the case, maybe I'm getting younger! But I came across a quote recently which said:

'Be Kind. Everyone is fighting a tough battle.'

I sense more people are facing difficulties than I'd perhaps been aware of. Yet when I share some of my challenges, people seem more willing to talk about their own. It's been good for me to take off the mask of self-sufficiency and I've found that honesty and openness can sometimes bring healing and reconciliation.

Going back to my health problems, it's better news. It's nothing serious. That's a relief, but it caused me to reflect on my priorities once again. At some stage I will depart this planet and so I want to give attention to the legacy I leave in terms of my relationships with others.

What will be your relationship legacy?

My friend John recently included the following words in an email he sent me. 'We don't always know that we've helped someone else ...' It reminded me that my attitudes and actions have consequences and repercussions that can be far wider than I might appreciate. They can impact and influence people that I may not even have direct contact with.

Just as a small stone can cause big ripples in a pond, so our actions have a ripple effect on others. You cannot get away from relationship ripples. Our actions and the choices we make are never in complete isolation – to a lesser or greater extent, they do ultimately impact other people's lives.

Such thoughts both challenge and inspire me.

Act4Africa is a charity I've had the privilege of working with. They work in Africa, educating and helping people with AIDS. A statement they often use on their publicity is, '*What we do in life echoes in eternity.*' These words resonate with my own values and beliefs – what I do today affects not just my tomorrow, but also the tomorrows of others. It boils down to this – in terms of relationships, what you and I do and say on a daily basis is creating a legacy.

Ebenezer Scrooge, the character in Charles Dickens' classic story *A Christmas Carol*, had the privilege of glimpsing into the future to see what legacy he would leave. In terms of money, he was wealthy, but in terms of meaningful, fulfilling relationships, he was poverty-stricken. If things remain the way they currently are in your life, how will you be remembered by others? Scrooge had the chance to change – he created a different relationship legacy. Will you?

At your funeral, most people will feel compelled to say something nice about you, but what I'm interested in would be what they would actually be thinking inside their heads. If they could be completely honest, what words would they really use to describe you? I'm conscious that unless I make changes in how I'm living my life, my two children, in the midst of a few positive comments, would also say 'bossy' and 'not around enough'.

What about you? What do people really think of you? If you were to leave this planet unexpectedly, how satisfied would you be with the memories colleagues, clients, friends and family would have of you? What can you take from this book that will help you create even better memories?

Is there a relationship that can be restored or renewed?

Is there someone who you need to contact today and decide to put the past behind you and move on to a better tomorrow?

Do you need to take an honest look at yourself and reflect on how you may have contributed to some of your relationship challenges?

Do you need to thank someone for the wonderful memories they've already given you?

Scrooge created a positive legacy because of the changes he made. It's a lesson for us all. Wishful thinking won't create the future we want – only action will. I sincerely hope that from this book, some idea or insight will have inspired you to take action that will improve the quality of your relationships. Never lose hope – tomorrow can be different from today – if you want it to be.

Hope SUMO makes a difference.

Paul McGee – The SUMO Guy

What Was Your SUMO Takeaway?

Speakers and writers thrive on feedback – and I'm no different. If you have some feedback about what you've read, then please feel free to email me at sumo@paulmcgee.com. I can assure you that, despite the vast amount of emails I receive from readers, I do personally read every single one. By giving me feedback, I'll ensure you receive my monthly newsletter, which aims to provide you with some further insights and ideas around my SUMO philosophy and also hopefully raise the occasional smile.

I look forward to hearing from you.

Paul McGee

Bring the SUMO Guy to Your Organisation

Paul McGee speaks at team events and conferences, as well as conducting workshops and retreats. He tailors his SUMO philosophy to your specific requirements, primarily in the areas of:

- Leadership;

- Motivation;

- Stress;

- Customer service;

- Relationships; and

- Succeeding through change.

In order to make contact with Paul McGee:

Email   sumo@paulmcgee.com

Visit   www.TheSumoGuy.com
          OR
          www.PaulMcGee.com

Telephone +44 (0) 1925 268708

Write to   20 Delphfields Road
          Appleton
          Warrington
          Cheshire
          WA4 5BY
          UK

Overview of the Six SUMO Principles

My previous book, *SUMO (Shut Up, Move On)*, explored six SUMO principles. Let me briefly recap on them in the context of relationships:

Principle one — change your T-shirt

Some people for whatever reason, have 'chosen' to wear the 'victim T-shirt'. It might not be a conscious decision, they may be unaware they're wearing it, but the reality of their action is clear. They believe that life is something that happens to you – we have little or no influence over it. We must accept the inevitable. What often happens in terms of relationships is due to luck or fate.

Their language is that of a victim, with no sense of control over their life – 'I've never been lucky in love.' 'I always end up with a difficult boss.' 'People always treat me badly, that's how it's always been.' A victim's life becomes a self-fulfilling prophecy. Their behaviour encourages people to treat them in a particular way. If they want to improve the quality of their relationships, they must learn to ditch the Victim T-Shirt mentality and start to take responsibility and control of their actions.

Principle two — develop 'fruity thinking'

The simple model I developed for this principle is **TEAR**: **T**hinking, **E**motions, **A**ctions, **R**esults. How I **t**hink and feel (my **e**motions) about myself, my life and the people I deal with, influences how I **a**ct and behave. Ultimately the quality of our lives (the '**r**esults') is influenced by how I think. Unfortunately the conversations inside our heads (that frequently are expressed outwardly) are not always helpful or constructive. I refer to these unhelpful conversations as 'faulty thinking' and identified four in particular.

Firstly, the one which seems to resonate the most wherever I speak in the world, the 'Inner Critic'. This is the voice that highlights your weaknesses and undermines your confidence.

The second is the 'Broken Record', where we get stuck in a certain way of unhelpful thinking. We delude ourselves into believing that continually thinking or talking about the problem will somehow resolve it.

Thirdly is the 'Martyr Syndrome', where our thinking convinces us that we are the victim. We dwell on feeling sorry for ourselves and focus on the unfairness of a situation, rather than resolving it.

Finally, we come to 'Trivial Pursuits', where our thinking dwells on trivial issues, that rationally speaking, are neither serious or important ... but we make them so.

These four types of faulty thinking are all interconnected (I can beat myself up over something trivial, feel sorry for myself and go on and on about it) and if left unchecked, can undermine how we interact with others. I devised seven simple but effective questions that are an antidote to faulty thinking and can lead us into 'fruity thinking', i.e. more fruitful outcomes (you can download these questions for free by going to www.TheSumoGuy.com/7questions.php).

Principle three — 'Hippo Time' is OK

We refer to this principle in more detail in this book. It's important to remember that sometimes, before we can move on, we need to recognise we may need time for a little wallowing (which reputedly is what hippos do in mud). Hippo Time is an opportunity to acknowledge your feelings and recognise that so-called negative emotions are not only valid, but also necessary if we are to function as healthy human beings.

Principle four — remember the beachball

This principle is so crucial and relevant to the area of relationships that I've decide to revisit it in more detail. If you've not read my first book yet, relax. I've devoted a whole chapter to re-examining this crucial insight.

Principle five — learn Latin

Based on the Latin phrase *'carpe diem'*, which translates as 'seize the day'. The bottom line? Life rewards action not intention. This book will throw up lots of great ideas, but their impact on your relationships will come not from reading about them, but by doing something with them. You won't act on every idea or insight, but if for every ten you action only one, you'll still begin to see some results.

Principle six — ditch Doris Day

Based on the song sung by Doris Day *'Que Sera, Sera,* Whatever will be will be'. This principle encourages us to take a more proactive approach to our lives.

Good relationships don't just happen – they are built and maintained. High morale within an organisation is not a question of luck, but is based upon a series of actions, principles, values and initiatives. Likewise, future success in any area of life stems from the actions you take on a daily basis.

These actions by themselves may not seem important, but they add up. The quality of your relationships is not at the mercy of what time of the year you were born or what some horoscope states will happen. It's based upon the choices you consistently make.

It might be convenient to leave things to chance and hope for the best, but as a long term strategy, it stinks. We don't apply this *'que sera sera'* attitude to other areas of our lives – so why should we leave perhaps the most important aspect of life – our relationships – to chance? It's in everyone's interests that relationships work well, so let's ditch, 'Whatever will be, will be' and start working towards the future we want to see.

So that's a brief catch up on the six SUMO principles and how they relate to relationships.

The Seven SUMO Questions

1 Where is this issue on a scale of 1–10? (10 = death)

2 How important will it be in six months time?

3 Is my response appropriate and effective?

4 How can I influence or improve the situation?

5 What can I learn from this?

6 What will I do differently next time?

7 What can I find that's positive in this situation?

Index